WASHINGTON AND HIS COMRADES IN ARMS

A CHRONICLE OF THE WAR OF INDEPENDENCE
BY GEORGE M. WRONG

NEW HAVEN: YALE UNIVERSITY PRESS
TORONTO: GLASGOW, BROOK & CO.
LONDON: HUMPHREY MILFORD
OXFORD UNIVERSITY PRESS

PREFATORY NOTE

THE author is aware of a certain audacity in undertaking, himself a Briton, to appear in a company of American writers on American history and above all to write on the subject of Washington. If excuse is needed it is to be found in the special interest of the career of Washington to a citizen of the British Commonwealth of Nations at the present time and in the urgency with which the editor and publishers declared that such an interpretation would not be unwelcome to Americans and pressed upon the author a task for which he doubted his own qualifications. To the editor he owes thanks for wise criticism. He is also indebted to Mr. Worthington Chauncey Ford, of the Massachusetts Historical Society, a great authority on Washington, who has kindly read the proofs and given helpful comments. Needless to say the author alone is responsible for opinions in the book.

UNIVERSITY OF TORONTO,
June 15, 1920.

CONTENTS

I. THE COMMANDER-IN-CHIEF   Page   1

II. BOSTON AND QUEBEC   "   27

III. INDEPENDENCE   "   54

IV. THE LOSS OF NEW YORK   "   81

V. THE LOSS OF PHILADELPHIA   "   108

VI. THE FIRST GREAT BRITISH DIS-
ASTER   "   123

VII. WASHINGTON AND HIS COMRADES
AT VALLEY FORGE   "   148

VIII. THE ALLIANCE WITH FRANCE AND
ITS RESULTS   "   182

IX. THE WAR IN THE SOUTH   "   211

X. FRANCE TO THE RESCUE   "   230

XI. YORKTOWN   "   247

BIBLIOGRAPHICAL NOTE   "   277

INDEX   "   283

WASHINGTON AND HIS COMRADES IN ARMS

∵

CHAPTER I

THE COMMANDER-IN-CHIEF

MOVING among the members of the second Continental Congress, which met at Philadelphia in May, 1775, was one, and but one, military figure. George Washington alone attended the sittings in uniform. This colonel from Virginia, now in his forty-fourth year, was a great landholder, an owner of slaves, an Anglican churchman, an aristocrat, everything that stands in contrast with the type of a revolutionary radical. Yet from the first he had been an outspoken and uncompromising champion of the colonial cause. When the tax was imposed on tea he had abolished the use of tea in his own household and when war was imminent he had talked of recruiting a thousand men at his own

1

expense and marching to Boston. His steady
wearing of the uniform seemed, indeed, to show
that he regarded the issue as hardly less military
than political.

The clash at Lexington, on the 19th of April,
had made vivid the reality of war. Passions ran
high. For years there had been tension, long disputes about buying British stamps to put on American legal papers, about duties on glass and paint
and paper and, above all, tea. Boston had shown
turbulent defiance, and to hold Boston down
British soldiers had been quartered on the inhabitants in the proportion of one soldier for five of the
populace, a great and annoying burden. And now
British soldiers had killed Americans who stood
barring their way on Lexington Green. Even calm
Benjamin Franklin spoke later of the hands of
British ministers as "red, wet, and dropping with
blood." Americans never forgot the fresh graves
made on that day. There were, it is true, more
British than American graves, but the British were
regarded as the aggressors. If the rest of the colonies were to join in the struggle, they must have
a common leader. Who should he be?

In June, while the Continental Congress faced
this question at Philadelphia, events at Boston

made the need of a leader more urgent. Boston was besieged by American volunteers under the command of General Artemas Ward. The siege had lasted for two months, each side watching the other at long range. General Gage, the British Commander, had the sea open to him and a finely tempered army upon which he could rely. The opposite was true of his opponents. They were a motley host rather than an army. They had few guns and almost no powder. Idle waiting since the fight at Lexington made untrained troops restless and anxious to go home. Nothing holds an army together like real war, and shrewd officers knew that they must give the men some hard task to keep up their fighting spirit. It was rumored that Gage was preparing an aggressive movement from Boston, which might mean pillage and massacre in the surrounding country, and it was decided to draw in closer to Boston to give Gage a diversion and prove the mettle of the patriot army. So, on the evening of June 16, 1775, there was a stir of preparation in the American camp at Cambridge, and late at night the men fell in near Harvard College.

Across the Charles River north from Boston, on a peninsula, lay the village of Charlestown, and rising behind it was Breed's Hill, about seventy-four feet high, extending northeastward to the higher elevation of Bunker Hill. The peninsula could be reached from Cambridge only by a narrow neck of land easily swept by British floating batteries lying off the shore. In the dark the American force of twelve hundred men under Colonel Prescott marched to this neck of land and then advanced half a mile southward to Breed's Hill. Prescott was an old campaigner of the Seven Years' War; he had six cannon, and his troops were commanded by experienced officers. Israel Putnam was skillful in irregular frontier fighting, and Nathanael Greene, destined to prove himself the best man in the American army next to Washington himself, could furnish sage military counsel derived from much thought and reading.

Thus it happened that on the morning of the 17th of June General Gage in Boston awoke to a surprise. He had refused to believe that he was shut up in Boston. It suited his convenience to stay there until a plan of campaign should be evolved by his superiors in London, but he was certain that when he liked he could, with his disciplined battalions, brush away the besieging army. Now he saw the American force on Breed's Hill throwing up a defiant and menacing redoubt and entrenchments. Gage did not hesitate. The bold aggressors must be driven away at once. He detailed for the enterprise William Howe, the officer destined soon to be his successor in the command at Boston. Howe was a brave and experienced soldier. He had been a friend of Wolfe and had led the party of twenty-four men who had first climbed the cliff at Quebec on the great day when Wolfe fell victorious. He was the younger brother of that beloved Lord Howe who had fallen at Ticonderoga and to whose memory Massachusetts had reared a monument in Westminster Abbey. Gage gave him in all some twenty-five hundred men, and, at about two in the afternoon, this force was landed at Charlestown.

The little town was soon aflame and the smoke helped to conceal Howe's movements. The day was boiling hot and the soldiers carried heavy packs with food for three days, for they intended to camp on Bunker Hill. Straight up Breed's Hill they marched wading through long grass sometimes to their knees and throwing down the fences on the hillside. The British knew that raw troops were likely to scatter their fire on a foe still out of range and they counted on a rapid bayonet charge against men helpless with empty rifles. This expectation was disappointed. The Americans had in front of them a barricade and Israel Putnam was there, threatening dire things to any one who should fire before he could see the whites of the eyes of the advancing soldiery. As the British came on there was a terrific discharge of musketry at twenty yards, repeated again and again as they either halted or drew back.

The slaughter was terrible. British officers hardened in war declared long afterward that they had never seen carnage like that of this fight. The American riflemen had been told to aim especially at the British officers, easily known by their uniforms, and one rifleman is said to have shot twenty officers before he was himself killed. Lord Rawdon, who played a considerable part in the war and was later, as Marquis of Hastings, Viceroy of India, used to tell of his terror as he fought in the British line. Suddenly a soldier was shot dead by his side, and, when he saw the man quiet at his feet, he said, "Is Death nothing but this?" and henceforth had no fear. When the first attack by the British was checked they retired; but, with dogged resolve, they re-formed and again charged up the hill, only a second time to be repulsed. The third time they

were more cautious. They began to work round
to the weaker defenses of the American left, where
there were no redoubts and entrenchments like
those on the right. By this time British ships were
throwing shells among the Americans. Charlestown was burning. The great column of black
smoke, the incessant roar of cannon, and the dreadful scenes of carnage had affected the defenders.
They wavered; and on the third British charge,
having exhausted their ammunition, they fled from
the hill in confusion back to the narrow neck of
land half a mile away, swept now by a British floating battery. General Burgoyne wrote that, in the
third attack, the discipline and courage of the
British private soldiers also broke down and that
when the redoubt was carried the officers of some
corps were almost alone. The British stood victorious at Bunker Hill. It was, however, a costly
victory. More than a thousand men, nearly half
of the attacking force, had fallen, with an undue
proportion of officers.

Philadelphia, far away, did not know what was
happening when, two days before the battle of
Bunker Hill, the Continental Congress settled the
question of a leader for a national army. On the

15th of June John Adams of Massachusetts rose
and moved that the Congress should adopt as its
own the army before Boston and that it should
name Washington as Commander-in-Chief. Adams
had deeply pondered the problem. He was certain
that New England would remain united and decided in the struggle, but he was not so sure of the
other colonies. To have a leader from beyond New
England would make for continental unity. Virginia, next to Massachusetts, had stood in the fore-
front of the movement, and Virginia was fortunate
in having in the Congress one whose fame as a soldier ran through all the colonies. There was something to be said for choosing a commander from the
colony which began the struggle and Adams knew
that his colleague from Massachusetts, John Hancock, a man of wealth and importance, desired the
post. He was conspicuous enough to be President
of the Congress. Adams says that when he made
his motion, naming a Virginian, he saw in Hancock's face "mortification and resentment." He
saw, too, that Washington hurriedly left the room
when his name was mentioned.

There could be no doubt as to what the Congress
would do. Unquestionably Washington was the
fittest man for the post. Twenty years earlier he

had seen important service in the war with France. His position and character commanded universal respect. The Congress adopted unanimously the motion of Adams and it only remained to be seen whether Washington would accept. On the next day he came to the sitting with his mind made up. The members, he said, would bear witness to his declaration that he thought himself unfit for the task. Since, however, they called him, he would try to do his duty. He would take the command but he would accept no pay beyond his expenses. Thus it was that Washington became a great national figure. The man who had long worn the King's uniform was now his deadliest enemy; and it is probably true that after this step nothing could have restored the old relations and reunited the British Empire. The broken vessel could not be made whole.

Washington spent only a few days in getting ready to take over his new command. On the 21st of June, four days after Bunker Hill, he set out from Philadelphia. The colonies were in truth very remote from each other. The journey to Boston was tedious. In the previous year John Adams had traveled in the other direction to the Congress at Philadelphia and, in his journal, he notes, as if he were traveling in foreign lands, the strange manners and customs of the other colonies. The journey, so momentous to Adams, was not new to Washington. Some twenty years earlier the young Virginian officer had traveled as far as Boston in the service of King George II. Now he was leader in the war against King George III. In New Jersey, New York, and Connecticut he was received impressively. In the warm summer weather the roads were good enough but many of the rivers were not bridged and could be crossed only by ferries or at fords. It took nearly a fortnight to reach Boston.

Washington had ridden only twenty miles on his long journey when the news reached him of the fight at Bunker Hill. The question which he asked anxiously shows what was in his mind: "Did the militia fight?" When the answer was "Yes," he said with relief, "The liberties of the country are safe." He reached Cambridge on the 2d of July and on the following day was the chief figure in a striking ceremony. In the presence of a vast crowd and of the motley army of volunteers, which was now to be called the American army, Washington assumed the command. He sat on horseback under an elm tree and an observer noted that his

appearance was "truly noble and majestic." This
was milder praise than that given a little later by
a London paper which said: "There is not a king
in Europe but would look like a *valet de chambre*
by his side." New England having seen him was
henceforth wholly on his side. His traditions were
not those of the Puritans, of the Ephraims and the
Abijahs of the volunteer army, men whose Old
Testament names tell something of the rigor of the
Puritan view of life. Washington, a sharer in the
free and often careless hospitality of his native
Virginia, had a different outlook. In his personal
discipline, however, he was not less Puritan than
the strictest of New Englanders. The coming
years were to show that a great leader had taken
his fitting place.

Washington, born in 1732, had been trained
in self-reliance, for he had been fatherless from
childhood. At the age of sixteen he was working
at the profession, largely self-taught, of a surveyor
of land. At the age of twenty-seven he married
Martha Custis, a rich widow with children, though
her marriage with Washington was childless. His
estate on the Potomac River, three hundred miles
from the open sea, recently named Mount Vernon,

had been in the family for nearly a hundred years. There were twenty-five hundred acres at Mount Vernon with ten miles of frontage on the tidal river. The Virginia planters were a landowning gentry; when Washington died he had more than sixty thousand acres. The growing of tobacco, the one vital industry of the Virginia of the time, with its half million people, was connected with the ownership of land. On their great estates the planters lived remote, with a mail perhaps every fortnight. There were no large towns, no great factories. Nearly half of the population consisted of negro slaves. It is one of the ironies of history that the chief leader in a war marked by a passion for liberty was a member of a society in which, as another of its members, Jefferson, the author of the Declaration of Independence, said, there was on the one hand the most insulting despotism and on the other the most degrading submission. The Virginian landowners were more absolute masters than the proudest lords of medieval England. These feudal lords had serfs on their land. The serfs were attached to the soil and were sold to a new master with the soil. They were not, however, property, without human rights. On the other hand, the slaves of the Virginian master were property like his horses. They could not even call wife and children their own, for these might be sold at will. It arouses a strange emotion now when we find Washington offering to exchange a negro for hogsheads of molasses and rum and writing that the man would bring a good price, "if kept clean and trim'd up a little when offered for sale."

In early life Washington had had very little of formal education. He knew no language but English. When he became world famous and his friend La Fayette urged him to visit France he refused because he would seem uncouth if unable to speak the French tongue. Like another great soldier, the Duke of Wellington, he was always careful about his dress. There was in him a silent pride which would brook nothing derogatory to his dignity. No one could be more methodical. He kept his accounts rigorously, entering even the cost of repairing a hairpin for a ward. He was a keen farmer, and it is amusing to find him recording in his careful journal that there are 844,800 seeds of "New River Grass" to the pound Troy and so determining how many should be sown to the acre. Not many youths would write out as did Washington, apparently from French sources, and read and reread elaborate "Rules of Civility and Decent

Behaviour in Company and Conversation." In the
fashion of the age of Chesterfield they portray the
perfect gentleman. He is always to remember the
presence of others and not to move, read, or speak
without considering what may be due to them. In
the true spirit of the time he is to learn to defer to
persons of superior quality. Tactless laughter at
his own wit, jests that have a sting of idle gossip,
are to be avoided. Reproof is to be given not in
anger but in a sweet and mild temper. The rules
descend even to manners at table and are a revela-
tion of care in self-discipline. We might imagine
Oliver Cromwell drawing up such rules, but not
Napoleon or Wellington.

The class to which Washington belonged prided
itself on good birth and good breeding. We picture
him as austere, but, like Oliver Cromwell, whom
in some respects he resembles, he was very human
in his personal relations. He liked a glass of wine.
He was fond of dancing and he went to the theater,
even on Sunday. He was, too, something of a
lady's man; "He can be downright impudent sometimes," wrote a Southern lady, "such impudence,
Fanny, as you and I like." In old age he loved to
have the young and gay about him. He could
break into furious oaths and no one was a better

master of what we may call honorable guile in
dealing with wily savages, in circulating falsehoods
that would deceive the enemy in time of war, or in
pursuing a business advantage. He played cards
for money and carefully entered loss and gain in
his accounts. He loved horseracing and horses,
and nothing pleased him more than to talk of that
noble animal. He kept hounds and until his burden
of cares became too great was an eager devotee of
hunting. His shooting was of a type more heroic
than that of an English squire spending a day on a
moor with guests and gamekeepers and returning
to comfort in the evening. Washington went off
on expeditions into the forest lasting many days
and shared the life in the woods of rough men,
sleeping often in the open air. "Happy," he wrote,
"is he who gets the berth nearest the fire." He
could spend a happy day in admiring the trees and
the richness of the land on a neighbor's estate.
Always his thoughts were turning to the soil.
There was poetry in him. It was said of Napoleon
that the one approach to poetry in all his writings
is the phrase: "The spring is at last appearing and
the leaves are beginning to sprout." Washington,
on the other hand, brooded over the mysteries of
life. He pictured to himself the serenity of a calm

old age and always dared to look death squarely in
the face. He was sensitive to human passion and
he felt the wonder of nature in all her ways, her
bounteous response in growth to the skill of man,
the delight of improving the earth in contrast with
the vain glory gained by ravaging it in war. His
most striking characteristics were energy and decision united often with strong likes and dislikes.
His clever secretary, Alexander Hamilton, found,
as he said, that his chief was not remarkable for
good temper and resigned his post because of an
impatient rebuke. When a young man serving
in the army of Virginia, Washington had many a
tussle with the obstinate Scottish Governor, Dinwiddie, who thought his vehemence unmannerly
and ungrateful. Gilbert Stuart, who painted several of his portraits, said that his features showed
strong passions and that, had he not learned self-
restraint, his temper would have been savage.
This discipline he acquired. The task was not easy,
but in time he was able to say with truth, "I have
no resentments," and his self-control became so
perfect as to be almost uncanny.

The assumption that Washington fought against
an England grown decadent is not justified. To
admit this would be to make his task seem lighter

than it really was. No doubt many of the rich aristocracy spent idle days of pleasure-seeking with
the comfortable conviction that they could discharge their duties to society by merely existing,
since their luxury made work and the more they
indulged themselves the more happy and profitable
employment would their many dependents enjoy.
The eighteenth century was, however, a wonderful
epoch in England. Agriculture became a new thing
under the leadership of great landowners like Lord
Townshend and Coke of Norfolk. Already was
abroad in society a divine discontent at existing
abuses. It brought Warren Hastings to trial on
the charge of plundering India. It attacked slavery, the cruelty of the criminal law, which sent
children to execution for the theft of a few pennies,
the brutality of the prisons, the torpid indifference
of the church to the needs of the masses. New
inventions were beginning the age of machinery.
The reform of Parliament, votes for the toiling
masses, and a thousand other improvements were
being urged. It was a vigorous, rich, and arrogant
England which Washington confronted.

It is sometimes said of Washington that he was
an English country gentleman. A gentleman he
was, but with an experience and training quite

2

unlike that of a gentleman in England. The young
heir to an English estate might or might not go to
a university. He could, like the young Charles
James Fox, become a scholar, but like Fox, who
knew some of the virtues and all the supposed
gentlemanly vices, he might dissipate his energies
in hunting, gambling, and cockfighting. He would
almost certainly make the grand tour of Europe,
and, if he had little Latin and less Greek, he was
pretty certain to have some familiarity with Paris
and a smattering of French. The eighteenth century was a period of magnificent living in England.
The great landowner, then, as now, the magnate
of his neighborhood, was likely to rear, if he did
not inherit, one of those vast palaces which are today burdens so costly to the heirs of their builders.
At the beginning of the century the nation to honor
Marlborough for his victories could think of nothing better than to give him half a million pounds
to build a palace. Even with the colossal wealth
produced by modern industry we should be stag-
gered at a residence costing millions of dollars.
Yet the Duke of Devonshire rivaled at Chats-
worth, and Lord Leicester at Holkham, Marlborough's building at Blenheim, and many other
costly palaces were erected during the following

half century. Their owners sometimes built in order to surpass a neighbor in grandeur, and to this day great estates are encumbered by the debts thus incurred in vain show. The heir to such a property was reared in a pomp and luxury undreamed of by the frugal young planter of Virginia. Of working for a livelihood, in the sense in which Washington knew it, the young Englishman of great estate would never dream.

The Atlantic is a broad sea and even in our own day, when instant messages flash across it and man himself can fly from shore to shore in less than a score of hours, it is not easy for those on one strand to understand the thought of those on the other. Every community evolves its own spirit not easily to be apprehended by the onlooker. The state of society in America was vitally different from that in England. The plain living of Virginia was in sharp contrast with the magnificence and ease of England. It is true that we hear of plate and elaborate furniture, of servants in livery, and much drinking of Port and Madeira, among the Virginians. They had good horses. Driving, as often they did, with six in a carriage, they seemed to keep up regal style. Spaces were wide in a country where one great landowner, Lord Fairfax, held no less than five million acres. Houses lay isolated and remote and a gentleman dining out would sometimes drive his elaborate equipage from twenty to fifty miles. There was a tradition of lavish hospitality, of gallant men and fair women, and sometimes of hard and riotous living. Many of the houses were, however, in a state of decay, with leaking roofs, battered doors and windows and shabby furniture. To own land in Virginia did not mean to live in luxurious ease. Land brought in truth no very large income. It was easier to break new land than to fertilize that long in use. An acre yielded only eight or ten bushels of wheat. In England the land was more fruitful. One who was only a tenant on the estate of Coke of Norfolk died worth £150,000, and Coke himself had the income of a prince. When Washington died he was reputed one of the richest men in America and yet his estate was hardly equal to that of Coke's tenant.

Washington was a good farmer, inventive and enterprising, but he had difficulties which ruined many of his neighbors. Today much of his infertile estate of Mount Vernon would hardly grow enough to pay the taxes. When Washington desired a gardener, or a bricklayer, or a carpenter, he usually had to buy him in the form of a convict, or of a negro slave, or of a white man indentured for a term of years. Such labor required eternal vigilance. The negro, himself property, had no respect for it in others. He stole when he could and worked only when the eyes of a master were upon him. If left in charge of plants or of stock he was likely to let them perish for lack of water. Washington's losses of cattle, horses, and sheep from this cause were enormous. The neglected cattle gave so little milk that at one time Washington, with a hundred cows, had to buy his butter. Negroes feigned sickness for weeks at a time. A visitor noted that Washington spoke to his slaves with a stern harshness. No doubt it was necessary. The management of this intractable material brought training in command. If Washington could make negroes efficient and farming pay in Virginia, he need hardly be afraid to meet any other type of difficulty.

From the first he was satisfied that the colonies had before them a difficult struggle. Many still refused to believe that there was really a state of war. Lexington and Bunker Hill might be regarded as unfortunate accidents to be explained away in an era of good feeling when each side should acknowledge the merits of the other and apologize for its own faults. Washington had few illusions of this kind. He took the issue in a serious and even bitter spirit. He knew nothing of the Englishman at home for he had never set foot outside of the colonies except to visit Barbados with an invalid half-brother. Even then he noted that the "gentleman inhabitants" whose "hospitality and genteel behaviour" he admired were discontented with the tone of the officials sent out from England. From early life Washington had seen much of British officers in America. Some of them had been men of high birth and station who treated the young colonial officer with due courtesy. When, however, he had served on the staff of the unfortunate General Braddock in the calamitous campaign of 1755, he had been offended by the tone of that leader. Probably it was in these days that Washington first brooded over the contrasts between the Englishman and the Virginian. With obstinate complacency Braddock had disregarded Washington's counsels of prudence. He showed arrogant confidence in his veteran troops and contempt for the amateur soldiers of whom Washington was one. In a wild country where rapid movement was the condition of success Braddock would

halt, as Washington said, "to level every mole hill
and to erect bridges over every brook." His transport was poor and Washington, a lover of horses,
chafed at what he called "vile management" of
the horses by the British soldier. When anything
went wrong Braddock blamed, not the ineffective
work of his own men, but the supineness of Virginia. "He looks upon the country," Washington
wrote in wrath, "I believe, as void of honour and
honesty." The hour of trial came in the fight of
July, 1755, when Braddock was defeated and killed
on the march to the Ohio. Washington told his
mother that in the fight the Virginian troops stood
their ground and were nearly all killed but the
boasted regulars "were struck with such a panic
that they behaved with more cowardice than it is
possible to conceive." In the anger and resentment of this comment is found the spirit which
made Washington a champion of the colonial cause
from the first hour of disagreement.

That was a fatal day in March, 1765, when the
British Parliament voted that it was just and
necessary that a revenue be raised in America.
Washington was uncompromising. After the tax
on tea he derided "our lordly masters in Great
Britain." No man, he said, should scruple for a

moment to take up arms against the threatened
tyranny. He and his neighbors of Fairfax County,
Virginia, took the trouble to tell the world by formal resolution on July 18, 1774, that they were
descended not from a conquered but from a con-
quering people, that they claimed full equality
with the people of Great Britain, and like them
would make their own laws and impose their own
taxes. They were not democrats; they had no
theories of equality; but as "gentlemen and men of
fortune" they would show to others the right path
in the crisis which had arisen. In this resolution
spoke the proud spirit of Washington; and, as he
brooded over what was happening, anger fortified
his pride. Of the Tories in Boston, some of them
highly educated men, who with sorrow were walk-
ing in what was to them the hard path of duty,
Washington could say later that "there never ex-
isted a more miserable set of beings than these
wretched creatures."

The age of Washington was one of bitter vehemence in political thought. In England the good
Whig was taught that to deny Whig doctrine was
blasphemy, that there was no truth or honesty on
the other side, and that no one should trust a Tory;
and usually the good Whig was true to the teaching

he had received. In America there had hitherto
been no national politics. Issues had been local
and passions thus confined exploded all the more
fiercely. Franklin spoke of George III as drinking
long draughts of American blood and of the British
people as so depraved and barbarous as to be the
wickedest nation upon earth, inspired by bloody
and insatiable malice and wickedness. To Washington George III was a tyrant, his ministers were
scoundrels, and the British people were lost to
every sense of virtue. The evil of it is that, for a
posterity which listened to no other comment on
the issues of the Revolution, such utterances, instead of being understood as passing expressions of
party bitterness, were taken as the calm judgments
of men held in reverence and awe. Posterity has
agreed that there is nothing to be said for the coerc-
ing of the colonies so resolutely pressed by George
III and his ministers. Posterity can also, however,
understand that the struggle was not between undiluted virtue on the one side and undiluted vice
on the other. Some eighty years after the American Revolution the Republic created by the Revolution endured the horrors of civil war rather
than accept its own disruption. In 1776 even the
most liberal Englishmen felt a similar passion for

the continued unity of the British Empire. Time has reconciled all schools of thought to the unity lost in the case of the Empire and to the unity preserved in the case of the Republic, but on the losing side in each case good men fought with deep conviction.

CHAPTER II

BOSTON AND QUEBEC

WASHINGTON was not a professional soldier, though he had seen the realities of war and had moved in military society. Perhaps it was an advantage that he had not received the rigid training of a regular, for he faced conditions which required an elastic mind. The force besieging Boston consisted at first chiefly of New England militia, with companies of minute-men, so called because of their supposed readiness to fight at a minute's notice. Washington had been told that he should find 20,000 men under his command; he found, in fact, a nominal army of 17,000, with probably not more than 14,000 effective, and the number tended to decline as the men went away to their homes after the first vivid interest gave way to the humdrum of military life.

The extensive camp before Boston, as Washington now saw it, expressed the varied character of his strange command. Cambridge, the seat of Harvard College, was still only a village with a few large houses and park-like grounds set among fields of grain, now trodden down by the soldiers. Here was placed in haphazard style the motley housing of a military camp. The occupants had followed their own taste in building. One could see structures covered with turf, looking like lumps of mother earth, tents made of sail cloth, huts of bare boards, huts of brick and stone, some having doors and windows of wattled basketwork. There were not enough huts to house the army nor camp-kettles for cooking. Blankets were so few that many of the men were without covering at night. In the warm summer weather this did not much matter but bleak autumn and harsh winter would bring bitter privation. The sick in particular suffered severely, for the hospitals were badly equipped.

A deep conviction inspired many of the volunteers. They regarded as brutal tyranny the tax on tea, considered in England as a mild expedient for raising needed revenue for defense in the colonies. The men of Suffolk County, Massachusetts, meeting in September, 1774, had declared in high-flown terms that the proposed tax came from a parricide who held a dagger at their bosoms and that those who resisted him would earn praises to eternity. From nearly every colony came similar utterances, and flaming resentment at injustice filled the volunteer army. Many a soldier would not touch a cup of tea because tea had been the ruin of his country. Some wore pinned to their hats or coats the words "Liberty or Death" and talked of resisting tyranny until "time shall be no more." It was a dark day for the motherland when so many of her sons believed that she was the enemy of liberty. The iron of this conviction entered into the soul of the American nation; at Gettysburg, nearly a century later, Abraham Lincoln, in a noble utterance which touched the heart of humanity, could appeal to the days of the Revolution, when "our fathers brought forth on this continent a new nation, conceived in liberty." The colonists believed that they were fighting for something of import to all mankind, and the nation which they created believes it still.

An age of war furnishes, however, occasion for the exercise of baser impulses. The New Englander was a trader by instinct. An army had come suddenly together and there was golden promise of contracts for supplies at fat profits.

The leader from Virginia, untutored in such things, was astounded at the greedy scramble. Before the year 1775 ended Washington wrote to his friend Lee that he prayed God he might never again have to witness such lack of public spirit, such jobbing and self-seeking, such "fertility in all the low arts," as now he found at Cambridge. He declared that if he could have foreseen all this nothing would have induced him to take the command. Later, the young La Fayette, who had left behind him in France wealth and luxury in order to fight a hard fight in America, was shocked at the slackness and indifference among the supposed patriots for whose cause he was making sacrifices so heavy. In the backward parts of the colonies the population was densely ignorant and had little grasp of the deeper meaning of the patriot cause.

The army was, as Washington himself said, "a mixed multitude." There was every variety of dress. Old uniforms, treasured from the days of the last French wars, had been dug out. A military coat or a cocked hat was the only semblance of uniform possessed by some of the officers. Rank was often indicated by ribbons of different colors tied on the arm. Lads from the farms had come in their usual dress; a good many of these were

hunters from the frontier wearing the buckskin of
the deer they had slain. Sometimes there was
clothing of grimmer material. Later in the war
an American officer recorded that his men had
skinned two dead Indians "from their hips down,
for bootlegs, one pair for the Major, the other for
myself." The volunteers varied greatly in age.
There were bearded veterans of sixty and a sprink-
ling of lads of sixteen. An observer laughed at
the boys and the "great great grandfathers" who
marched side by side in the army before Boston.
Occasionally a black face was seen in the ranks.
One of Washington's tasks was to reduce the dis-
parity of years and especially to secure men who
could shoot. In the first enthusiasm of 1775 so
many men volunteered in Virginia that a selection
was made on the basis of accuracy in shooting.
The men fired at a range of one hundred and fifty
yards at an outline of a man's nose in chalk on a
board. Each man had a single shot and the first
men shot the nose entirely away.

Undoubtedly there was the finest material
among the men lounging about their quarters at
Cambridge in fashion so unmilitary. In physique
they were larger than the British soldier, a result
due to abundant food and free life in the open air

from childhood. Most of the men supplied their own uniform and rifles and much barter went on in the hours after drill. The men made and sold shoes, clothes, and even arms. They were accustomed to farm life and good at digging and throwing up entrenchments. The colonial mode of waging war was, however, not that of Europe. To the regular soldier of the time even earth entrenchments seemed a sign of cowardice. The brave man would come out on the open to face his foe. Earl Percy, who rescued the harassed British on the day of Lexington, had the poorest possible opinion of those on what he called the rebel side. To him they were intriguing rascals, hypocrites, cowards, with sinister designs to ruin the Empire. But he was forced to admit that they fought well and faced death willingly.

In time Washington gathered about him a fine body of officers, brave, steady, and efficient. On the great issue they, like himself, had unchanging conviction, and they and he saved the revolution. But a good many of his difficulties were due to bad officers. He had himself the reverence for gentility, the belief in an ordered grading of society, characteristic of his class in that age. In Virginia the relation of master and servant was

well understood and the tone of authority was
readily accepted.   In New England conceptions
of equality were more advanced.   The extent to
which the people would brook the despotism of
military command was uncertain.   From the first
some of the volunteers had elected their officers.
The result was that intriguing demagogues were
sometimes chosen.   The Massachusetts troops,
wrote a Connecticut captain, not free, perhaps,
from local jealousy, were "commanded by a most
despicable set of officers."   At Bunker Hill officers
of this type shirked the fight and their men, left
without leaders, joined in the panicky retreat of
that day.   Other officers sent away soldiers to work
on their farms while at the same time they drew
for them public pay.   At a later time Washington
wrote to a friend wise counsel about the choice of
officers.   "Take none but gentlemen; let no local
attachment influence you; do not suffer your good
nature to say Yes when you ought to say No.
Remember that it is a public, not a private cause."
What he desired was the gentleman's chivalry of
refinement, sense of honor, dignity of character,
and freedom from mere self-seeking.   The prime
qualities of a good officer, as he often said, were
authority and decision.   It is probably true of

3

democracies that they prefer and will follow the man who will take with them a strong tone. Little men, however, cannot see this and think to gain support by shifty changes of opinion to please the multitude. What authority and decision could be expected from an officer of the peasant type, elected by his own men? How could he dominate men whose short term of service was expiring and who had to be coaxed to renew it? Some elected officers had to promise to pool their pay with that of their men. In one company an officer fulfilled the double position of captain and barber. In time, however, the authority of military rank came to be respected throughout the whole army. An amusing contrast with earlier conditions is found in 1779 when a captain was tried by a brigade court-martial and dismissed from the service for intimate association with the wagon-maker of the brigade.

The first thing to do at Cambridge was to get rid of the inefficient and the corrupt. Washington had never any belief in a militia army. From his earliest days as a soldier he had favored conscription, even in free Virginia. He had then found quite ineffective the "whooping, holloing gentlemen soldiers" of the volunteer force of the colony

among whom "every individual has his own crude
notion of things and must undertake to direct. If
his advice is neglected he thinks himself slighted,
abused, and injured and, to redress his wrongs, will
depart for his home." Washington found at Cambridge too many officers. Then as later in the
American army there were swarms of colonels.
The officers from Massachusetts, conscious that
they had seen the first fighting in the great cause,
expected special consideration from a stranger
serving on their own soil. Soon they had a rude
awakening. Washington broke a Massachusetts
colonel and two captains because they had proved
cowards at Bunker Hill, two more captains for
fraud in drawing pay and provisions for men who
did not exist, and still another for absence from his
post when he was needed. He put in jail a colonel,
a major, and three or four other officers. "New
lords, new laws," wrote in his diary Mr. Emerson,
the chaplain: "the Generals Washington and Lee
are upon the lines every day . . . great distinction
is made between officers and soldiers."

The term of all the volunteers in Washington's
army expired by the end of 1775, so that he had to
create a new army during the siege of Boston. He
spoke scornfully of an enemy so little enterprising

as to remain supine during the process. But probably the British were wise to avoid a venture
inland and to remain in touch with their fleet.
Washington made them uneasy when he drove
away the cattle from the neighborhood.   Soon beef
was selling in Boston for as much as eighteen pence
a pound.   Food might reach Boston in ships but
supplies even by sea were insecure, for the Americans soon had privateers manned by seamen familiar with New England waters and happy in expected gains from prize money.   The British were
anxious about the elementary problem of food.
They might have made Washington more uncom-
fortable by forays and alarms.   Only reluctantly,
however, did Howe, who took over the command
on October 10, 1775, admit to himself that this was
a real war.   He still hoped for settlement without
further bloodshed.   Washington was glad to learn
that the British were laying in supplies of coal for
the winter.   It meant that they intended to stay
in Boston, where, more than in any other place, he
could make trouble for them.

Washington had more on his mind than the creation of an army and the siege of Boston.   He had
also to decide the strategy of the war.   On the long
American sea front Boston alone remained in

British hands. New York, Philadelphia, Charleston and other ports farther south were all, for the time, on the side of the Revolution. Boston was not a good naval base for the British, since it commanded no great waterway leading inland. The sprawling colonies, from the rock-bound coast of New England to the swamps and forests of Georgia, were strong in their incoherent vastness. There were a thousand miles of seacoast. Only rarely were considerable settlements to be found more than a hundred miles distant from salt water. An army marching to the interior would have increasing difficulties from transport and supplies. Wherever water routes could be used the naval power of the British gave them an advantage. One such route was the Hudson, less a river than a navigable arm of the sea, leading to the heart of the colony of New York, its upper waters almost touching Lake George and Lake Champlain, which in turn led to the St. Lawrence in Canada and thence to the sea. Canada was held by the British; and it was clear that, if they should take the city of New York, they might command the whole line from the mouth of the Hudson to the St. Lawrence, and so cut off New England from the other colonies and overcome a divided enemy. To foil this policy

Washington planned to hold New York and to capture Canada. With Canada in line the union of the colonies would be indeed continental, and, if the British were driven from Boston, they would have no secure foothold in North America.

The danger from Canada had always been a source of anxiety to the English colonies. The French had made Canada a base for attempts to drive the English from North America. During many decades war had raged along the Canadian frontier. With the cession of Canada to Britain in 1763 this danger had vanished. The old habit endured, however, of fear of Canada. When, in 1774, the British Parliament passed the bill for the government of Canada known as the Quebec Act, there was violent clamor. The measure was assumed to be a calculated threat against colonial liberty. The Quebec Act continued in Canada the French civil law and the ancient privileges of the Roman Catholic Church. It guaranteed order in the wild western region north of the Ohio, taken recently from France, by placing it under the authority long exercised there of the Governor of Quebec. Only a vivid imagination would conceive that to allow to the French in Canada their old loved customs and laws involved designs against the freedom under

English law in the other colonies, or that to let the
Canadians retain in respect to religion what they
had always possessed meant a sinister plot against
the Protestantism of the English colonies. Yet
Alexander Hamilton, perhaps the greatest mind in
the American Revolution, had frantic suspicions.
French laws in Canada involved, he said, the extension of French despotism in the English colonies.
The privileges continued to the Roman Catholic
Church in Canada would be followed in due course
by the Inquisition, the burning of heretics at the
stake in Boston and New York, and the bringing
from Europe of Roman Catholic settlers who would
prove tools for the destruction of religious liberty.
Military rule at Quebec meant, sooner or later,
despotism everywhere in America. We may smile
now at the youthful Hamilton's picture of "dark
designs" and "deceitful wiles" on the part of
that fierce Protestant George III to establish
Roman Catholic despotism, but the colonies regarded the danger as serious. The quick remedy
would be simply to take Canada, as Washington
now planned.

To this end something had been done before
Washington assumed the command. The British
Fort Ticonderoga, on the neck of land separating

Lake Champlain from Lake George, commanded
the route from New York to Canada. The fight at
Lexington in April had been quickly followed by
aggressive action against this British stronghold.
No news of Lexington had reached the fort when
early in May Colonel Ethan Allen, with Benedict
Arnold serving as a volunteer in his force of eighty-
three men, arrived in friendly guise. The fort was
held by only forty-eight British; with the menace
from France at last ended they felt secure; discipline was slack, for there was nothing to do. The
incompetent commander testified that he lent Allen
twenty men for some rough work on the lake. By
evening Allen had them all drunk and then it was
easy, without firing a shot, to capture the fort with
a rush. The door to Canada was open. Great
stores of ammunition and a hundred and twenty
guns, which in due course were used against the
British at Boston, fell into American hands.

About Canada Washington was ill-informed.
He thought of the Canadians as if they were Virginians or New Yorkers. They had been recently
conquered by Britain; their new king was a tyrant; they would desire liberty and would welcome
an American army. So reasoned Washington,
but without knowledge. The Canadians were a

conquered people, but they had found the British king no tyrant and they had experienced the paradox of being freer under the conqueror than they had been under their own sovereign. The last days of French rule in Canada were disgraced by corruption and tyranny almost unbelievable. The Canadian peasant had been cruelly robbed and he had conceived for his French rulers a dislike which appears still in his attitude towards the motherland of France. For his new British master he had assuredly no love, but he was no longer dragged off to war and his property was not plundered. He was free, too, to speak his mind. During the first twenty years after the British conquest of Canada the Canadian French matured indeed an assertive liberty not even dreamed of during the previous century and a half of French rule.

The British tyranny which Washington pictured in Canada was thus not very real. He underestimated, too, the antagonism between the Roman Catholics of Canada and the Protestants of the English colonies. The Congress at Philadelphia in denouncing the Quebec Act had accused the Catholic Church of bigotry, persecution, murder, and rebellion. This was no very tactful appeal for sympathy to the sons of that France which was still the eldest daughter of the Church and it was hardly helped by a maladroit turn suggesting that "low-minded infirmities" should not permit such differences to block union in the sacred cause of liberty. Washington believed that two battalions of Canadians might be recruited to fight the British, and that the French Acadians of Nova Scotia, a people so remote that most of them hardly knew what the war was about, were tingling with sympathy for the American cause. In truth the Canadian was not prepared to fight on either side. What the priest and the landowner could do to make him fight for Britain was done, but, for all that, Sir Guy Carleton, the Governor of Canada, found recruiting impossible.

Washington believed that the war would be won by the side which held Canada. He saw that from Canada would be determined the attitude of the savages dwelling in the wild spaces of the interior; he saw, too, that Quebec as a military base in British hands would be a source of grave danger. The easy capture of Fort Ticonderoga led him to underrate difficulties. If Ticonderoga why not Quebec? Nova Scotia might be occupied later, the Acadians helping. Thus it happened that, soon after taking over the command, Washington was busy with a plan for the conquest of Canada. Two forces were to advance into that country; one by way of Lake Champlain under General Schuyler and the other through the forests of Maine under Benedict Arnold.

Schuyler was obliged through illness to give up his command, and it was an odd fortune of war that put General Richard Montgomery at the head of the expedition going by way of Lake Champlain. Montgomery had served with Wolfe at the taking of Louisbourg and had been an officer in the proud British army which had received the surrender of Canada in 1760. Not without searching of heart had Montgomery turned against his former sovereign. He was living in America when war broke out; he had married into an American family of position; and he had come to the view that vital liberty was challenged by the King. Now he did his work well, in spite of very bad material in his army. His New Englanders were, he said, "every man a general and not one of them a soldier." They feigned sickness, though, as far as he had learned, there was "not a man dead of any distemper." No better were the men from New York, "the sweepings of the streets" with morals "infamous." Of the officers, too, Montgomery had a poor opinion. Like Washington he declared that it was necessary to get gentlemen, men of education and integrity, as officers, or disaster would follow. Nevertheless St. Johns, a British post on the Richelieu, about thirty miles across country from Montreal, fell to Montgomery on the 3d of November, after a siege of six weeks; and British regulars under Major Preston, a brave and competent officer, yielded to a crude volunteer army with whole regiments lacking uniforms. Montreal could make no defense. On the 12th of November Montgomery entered Montreal and was in control of the St. Lawrence almost to the cliffs of Quebec. Canada seemed indeed an easy conquest.

The adventurous Benedict Arnold went on an expedition more hazardous. He had persuaded Washington of the impossible, that he could advance through the wilderness from the seacoast of Maine and take Quebec by surprise. News travels even by forest pathways. Arnold made a wonderful effort. Chill autumn was upon him when, on the 25th of September, with about a thousand picked men, he began to advance up the Kennebec River and over the height of land to the upper waters of the Chaudière, which discharges into the St. Lawrence opposite Quebec. There were heavy rains. Sometimes the men had to wade breast high in dragging heavy and leaking boats over the difficult places. A good many men died of starvation. Others deserted and turned back. The indomitable Arnold pressed on, however, and on the 9th of November, a few days before Montgomery occupied Montreal, he stood with some six hundred worn and shivering men on the strand of the St. Lawrence opposite Quebec. He had not surprised the city and it looked grim and inaccessible as he surveyed it across the great river. In the autumn gales it was not easy to carry over his little army in small boats. But this he accomplished and then waited for Montgomery to join him.

By the 3d of December Montgomery was with Arnold before Quebec. They had hardly more than a thousand effective troops, together with a few hundred Canadians, upon whom no reliance could be placed. Carleton, commanding at Quebec, sat tight and would hold no communication with despised "rebels." "They all pretend to be gentlemen," said an astonished British officer in Quebec, when he heard that among the American officers now captured by the British there were a former blacksmith, a butcher, a shoemaker, and an innkeeper. Montgomery was stung to violent threats by Carleton's contempt, but never could he draw from Carleton a reply. At last Montgomery tried, in the dark of early morning of New Year's Day, 1776, to carry Quebec by storm. He was to lead an attack on the Lower Town from the west side, while Arnold was to enter from the opposite side. When they met in the center they were to storm the citadel on the heights above. They counted on the help of the French inhabitants, from whom Carleton said bitterly enough that he had nothing to fear in prosperity and nothing to hope for in adversity. Arnold pressed his part of the attack with vigor and penetrated to the streets of the Lower Town where he fell wounded. Captain Daniel Morgan, who took over the command, was made prisoner.

Montgomery's fate was more tragic. In spite of protests from his officers, he led in person the attack from the west side of the fortress. The advance was along a narrow road under the towering cliffs of a great precipice. The attack was expected by the British and the guard at the barrier was ordered to hold its fire until the enemy was near. Suddenly there was a roar of cannon and the assailants not swept down fled in panic. With the morning light the dead head of Montgomery was

found protruding from the snow. He was mourned
by Washington and with reason. He had talents
and character which might have made him one
of the chief leaders of the revolutionary army.
Elsewhere, too, was he mourned. His father, an
Irish landowner, had been a member of the British
Parliament, and he himself was a Whig, known to
Fox and Burke. When news of his death reached
England eulogies upon him came from the Whig
benches in Parliament which could not have been
stronger had he died fighting for the King.

While the outlook in Canada grew steadily
darker, the American cause prospered before Boston. There Howe was not at ease. If it was really
to be war, which he still doubted, it would be
well to seek some other base. Washington helped
Howe to take action. Dorchester Heights commanded Boston as critically from the south as did
Bunker Hill from the north. By the end of February Washington had British cannon, brought
with heavy labor from Ticonderoga, and then he
lost no time. On the morning of March 5, 1776,
Howe awoke to find that, under cover of a heavy
bombardment, American troops had occupied Dorchester Heights and that if he would dislodge

them he must make another attack similar to that at Bunker Hill. The alternative of stiff fighting was the evacuation of Boston. Howe, though dilatory, was a good fighting soldier. His defects as a general in America sprang in part from his belief that the war was unjust and that delay might bring counsels making for peace and save bloodshed. His first decision was to attack, but a furious gale thwarted his purpose, and he then prepared for the inevitable step.

Washington divined Howe's purpose and there was a tacit agreement that the retiring army should not be molested. Howe destroyed munitions of war which he could not take away but he left intact the powerful defenses of Boston, defenses reared at the cost of Britain. Many of the better class of the inhabitants, British in their sympathies, were now face to face with bitter sorrow and sacrifice. Passions were so aroused that a hard fate awaited them should they remain in Boston and they decided to leave with the British army. Travel by land was blocked; they could go only by sea. When the time came to depart, laden carriages, trucks, and wheelbarrows crowded to the quays through the narrow streets and a sad procession of exiles went out from their homes. A profane critic said that they moved "as if the very devil was after them." No doubt many of them would have been arrogant and merciless to "rebels" had theirs been the triumph. But the day was above all a day of sorrow. Edward Winslow, a strong leader among them, tells of his tears "at leaving our once happy town of Boston." The ships, a forest of masts, set sail and, crowded with soldiers and refugees, headed straight out to sea for Halifax. Abigail, wife of John Adams, a clever woman, watched the departure of the fleet with gladness in her heart. She thought that never before had been seen in America so many ships bearing so many people. Washington's army marched joyously into Boston. Joyous it might well be since, for the moment, powerful Britain was not secure in a single foot of territory in the former colonies. If Quebec should fall the continent would be almost conquered.

Quebec did not fall. All through the winter the Americans held on before the place. They shivered from cold. They suffered from the dread disease of smallpox. They had difficulty in getting food. The Canadians were insistent on having good money for what they offered and since good money was not always in the treasury the invading army

4

sometimes used violence.   Then the Canadians became more reserved and chilling than ever.   In hope of mending matters Congress sent a commission to Montreal in the spring of 1776.   Its chairman was Benjamin Franklin and, with him, were two leading Roman Catholics, Charles Carroll of Carrollton, a great landowner of Maryland, and his brother John, a priest, afterwards Archbishop of Baltimore.   It was not easy to represent as the liberator of the Catholic Canadians the Congress which had denounced in scathing terms the concessions in the Quebec Act to the Catholic Church.   Franklin was a master of conciliation, but before he achieved anything a dramatic event happened.   On the 6th of May, British ships arrived at Quebec.   The inhabitants rushed to the ramparts.   Cries of joy passed from street to street and they reached the little American army, now under General Thomas, encamped on the Plains of Abraham.   Panic seized the small force which had held on so long.   On the ships were ten thousand fresh British troops.   The one thing for the Americans to do was to get away; and they fled, leaving behind guns, supplies, even clothing and private papers.   Five days later Franklin, at Montreal, was dismayed by the distressing news of disaster.

Congress sent six regiments to reinforce the army which had fled from Quebec. It was a desperate venture. Washington's orders were that the Americans should fight the new British army as near Quebec as possible. The decisive struggle took place on the 8th of June. An American force under the command of General Thompson attacked Three Rivers, a town on the St. Lawrence, half way between Quebec and Montreal. They were repulsed and the general was taken prisoner. The wonder is indeed that the army was not annihilated. Then followed a disastrous retreat. Short of supplies, ravaged by smallpox, and in bad weather, the invaders tried to make their way back to Lake Champlain. They evacuated Montreal. It is hard enough in the day of success to hold together an untrained army. In the day of defeat such a force is apt to become a mere rabble. Some of the American regiments preserved discipline. Others fell into complete disorder as, weak and discouraged, they retired to Lake Champlain. Many soldiers perished of disease. "I did not look into a hut or a tent," says an observer, "in which I did not find a dead or dying man." Those who had huts were fortunate. The fate of some was to die without medical care and without cover. By the end of June what was left of the force had reached Crown Point on Lake Champlain.

Benedict Arnold, who had been wounded at Quebec, was now at Crown Point. Competent critics of the war have held that what Arnold now did saved the Revolution. In another scene, before the summer ended, the British had taken New York and made themselves masters of the lower Hudson. Had they reached in the same season the upper Hudson by way of Lake Champlain they would have struck blows doubly staggering. This Arnold saw, and his object was to delay, if he could not defeat, the British advance. There was no road through the dense forest by the shores of Lake Champlain and Lake George to the upper Hudson. The British must go down the lake in boats. This General Carleton had foreseen and he had urged that with the fleet sent to Quebec should be sent from England, in sections, boats which could be quickly carried past the rapids of the Richelieu River and launched on Lake Champlain. They had not come and the only thing for Carleton to do was to build a flotilla which could carry an army up the lake and attack Crown Point. The thing was done but skilled workmen were few and not until the 5th of October were the little ships afloat

on Lake Champlain. Arnold, too, spent the summer in building boats to meet the attack and it
was a strange turn in warfare which now made him
commander in a naval fight. There was a brisk
struggle on Lake Champlain. Carleton had a score
or so of vessels; Arnold not so many. But he delayed Carleton. When he was beaten on the water
he burned the ships not captured and took to the
land. When he could no longer hold Crown Point
he burned that place and retreated to Ticonderoga.

By this time it was late autumn. The British
were far from their base and the Americans were
retreating into a friendly country. There is little
doubt that Carleton could have taken Fort Ticonderoga. It fell quite easily less than a year later.
Some of his officers urged him to press on and do it.
But the leaves had already fallen, the bleak winter
was near, and Carleton pictured to himself an
army buried deeply in an enemy country and
separated from its base by many scores of miles of
lake and forest. He withdrew to Canada and left
Lake Champlain to the Americans.

CHAPTER III

INDEPENDENCE

WELL-MEANING people in England found it difficult to understand the intensity of feeling in America. Britain had piled up a huge debt in driving France from America. Landowners were paying in taxes no less than twenty per cent of their incomes from land. The people who had chiefly benefited by the humiliation of France were the colonists, now freed from hostile menace and secure for extension over a whole continent. Why should not they pay some share of the cost of their own security? Certain facts tended to make Englishmen indignant with the Americans. Every effort had failed to get them to pay willingly for their defense. Before the Stamp Act had become law in 1765 the colonies were given a whole year to devise the raising of money in any way which they liked better. The burden of what was asked would be light. Why should not they agree to bear it? Why this talk, repeated by the Whigs in the British Parliament, of brutal tyranny, oppression, hired minions imposing slavery, and so on. Where were the oppressed? Could any one point to a single person who before war broke out had known British tyranny? What suffering could any one point to as the result of the tax on tea? The people of England paid a tax on tea four times heavier than that paid in America. Was not the British Parliament supreme over the whole Empire? Did not the colonies themselves admit that it had the right to control their trade overseas? And if men shirk their duty should they not come under some law of compulsion?

It was thus that many a plain man reasoned in England. The plain man in America had his own opposing point of view. Debts and taxes in England were not his concern. He remembered the recent war as vividly as did the Englishman, and, if the English paid its cost in gold, he had paid his share in blood and tears. Who made up the armies led by the British generals in America? More than half the total number who served in America came from the colonies, the colonies which had barely a third of the population of Great Britain. True, Britain paid the bill in money but why not? She was rich with a vast accumulated capital. The war, partly in America, had given her the key to the wealth of India.   Look at the magnificence, the pomp of servants, plate and pictures, the parks and gardens, of hundreds of English country houses, and compare this opulence with the simple mode of life, simplicity imposed by necessity, of a country gentleman like George Washington of Virginia, reputed to be the richest man in America.   Thousands of tenants in England, owning no acre of land, were making a larger income than was possible in America to any owner of broad acres.   It was true that America had gained from the late war.   The foreign enemy had been struck down. But had he not been struck down too for England? Had there not been far more dread in England of invasion by France and had not the colonies by helping to ruin France freed England as much as England had freed them?   If now the colonies were asked to pay a share of the bill for the British army that was a matter for discussion.   They had never before done it and they must not be told that they had to meet the demand within a year or be compelled to pay.   Was it not to impose tyranny and slavery to tell a people that their property would be taken by force if they did not choose to give it,

What free man would not rather die than yield on such a point?

The familiar workings of modern democracy have taught us that a great political issue must be discussed in broad terms of high praise or severe blame. The contestants will exaggerate both the virtue of the side they espouse and the malignity of the opposing side; nice discrimination is not possible. It was inevitable that the dispute with the colonies should arouse angry vehemence on both sides. The passionate speech of Patrick Henry in Virginia, in 1763, which made him famous, and was the forerunner of his later appeal, "Give me Liberty or give me Death," related to so prosaic a question as the right of disallowance by England of an act passed by a colonial legislature, a right exercised long and often before that time and to this day a part of the constitutional machinery of the British Empire. Few men have lived more serenely poised than Washington, yet, as we have seen, he hated the British with an implacable hatred. He was a humane man. In earlier years, Indian raids on the farmers of Virginia had stirred him to "deadly sorrow," and later, during his retreat from New York, he was moved by the cries of the weak and infirm. Yet the same man felt no

touch of pity for the Loyalists of the Revolution.
To him they were detestable parricides, vile traitors, with no right to live. When we find this note
in Washington, in America, we hardly wonder that
the high Tory, Samuel Johnson, in England, should
write that the proposed taxation was no tyranny,
that it had not been imposed earlier because "we
do not put a calf into the plough; we wait till he is
an ox," and that the Americans were "a race of
convicts, and ought to be thankful for anything
which we allow them short of hanging." Tyranny
and treason are both ugly things. Washington
believed that he was fighting the one, Johnson that
he was fighting the other, and neither side would
admit the charge against itself.

Such are the passions aroused by civil strife.
We need not now, when they are, or ought to be,
dead, spend any time in deploring them. It suffices
to explain them and the events to which they led.
There was one and really only one final issue.
Were the American colonies free to govern themselves as they liked or might their government in
the last analysis be regulated by Great Britain?
The truth is that the colonies had reached a condition in which they regarded themselves as British states with their own parliaments, exercising

complete jurisdiction in their own affairs. They intended to use their own judgment and they were as restless under attempted control from England as England would have been under control from America. We can indeed always understand the point of view of Washington if we reverse the position and imagine what an Englishman would have thought of a claim by America to tax him.

An ancient and proud society is reluctant to change. After a long and successful war England was prosperous. To her now came riches from India and the ends of the earth. In society there was such lavish expenditure that Horace Walpole declared an income of twenty thousand pounds a year was barely enough. England had an aristocracy the proudest in the world, for it had not only rank but wealth. The English people were certain of the invincible superiority of their nation. Every Englishman was taught, as Disraeli said of a later period, to believe that he occupied a position better than any one else of his own degree in any other country in the world. The merchant in England was believed to surpass all others in wealth and integrity, the manufacturer to have no rivals in skill, the British sailor to stand in a class by himself, the British officer to express the last word in

chivalry. It followed, of course, that the motherland was superior to her children overseas. The
colonies had no aristocracy, no great landowners
living in stately palaces. They had almost no
manufactures. They had no imposing state system with places and pensions from which the fortunate might reap a harvest of ten or even twenty
thousand pounds a year. They had no ancient
universities thronged by gilded youth who, if noble,
might secure degrees without the trying ceremony
of an examination. They had no Established
Church with the ancient glories of its cathedrals.
In all America there was not even a bishop. In
spite of these contrasts the English Whigs insisted
upon the political equality with themselves of
the American colonists. The Tory squire, however, shared Samuel Johnson's view that colonists
were either traders or farmers and that colonial
shopkeeping society was vulgar and contemptible.

George III was ill-fitted by nature to deal with
the crisis. The King was not wholly without
natural parts, for his own firm will had achieved
what earlier kings had tried and failed to do; he
had mastered Parliament, made it his obedient
tool and himself for a time a despot. He had some
admirable virtues. He was a family man, the

father of fifteen children. He liked quiet amusements and had wholesome tastes. If industry and
belief in his own aims could of themselves make a
man great we might reverence George. He wrote
once to Lord North: "I have no object but to be
of use: if that is ensured I am completely happy."
The King was always busy. Ceaseless industry
does not, however, include every virtue, or the
author of all evil would rank high in goodness.
Wisdom must be the pilot of good intentions.
George was not wise. He was ill-educated. He
had never traveled. He had no power to see the
point of view of others.

As if nature had not sufficiently handicapped
George for a high part, fate placed him on the
throne at the immature age of twenty-two. Henceforth the boy was master, not pupil. Great nobles
and obsequious prelates did him reverence. Ignorant and obstinate, the young King was determined
not only to reign but to rule, in spite of the new
doctrine that Parliament, not the King, carried
on the affairs of government through the leader of
the majority in the House of Commons, already
known as the Prime Minister. George could not
really change what was the last expression of political forces in England. The rule of Parliament

had come to stay. Through it and it alone could the realm be governed. This power, however, though it could not be destroyed, might be controlled. Parliament, while retaining all its privileges, might yet carry out the wishes of the sovereign. The King might be his own Prime Minister. The thing could be done if the King's friends held a majority of the seats and would do what their master directed. It was a dark day for England when a king found that he could play off one faction against another, buy a majority in Parliament, and retain it either by paying with guineas or with posts and dignities which the bought Parliament left in his gift. This corruption it was which ruined the first British Empire.

We need not doubt that George thought it his right and also his duty to coerce America, or rather, as he said, the clamorous minority which was trying to force rebellion. He showed no lack of sincerity. On October 26, 1775, while Washington was besieging Boston, he opened Parliament with a speech which at any rate made the issue clear enough. Britain would not give up colonies which she had founded with severe toil and nursed with great kindness. Her army and her navy, both now increased in size, would make her power respected.

She would not, however, deal harshly with her
erring children. Royal mercy would be shown to
those who admitted their error and they need not
come to England to secure it. Persons in America
would be authorized to grant pardons and furnish the guarantees which would proceed from the
royal clemency.

Such was the magnanimity of George III.
Washington's rage at the tone of the speech is
almost amusing in its vehemence. He, with a
mind conscious of rectitude and sacrifice in a great
cause, to ask pardon for his course! He to bend
the knee to this tyrant overseas! Washington
himself was not highly gifted with imagination.
He never realized the strength of the forces in
England arrayed on his own side and attributed
to the English, as a whole, sinister and malignant
designs always condemned by the great mass of
the English people. They, no less than the Americans, were the victims of a turn in politics which,
for a brief period, and for only a brief period, left
power in the hands of a corrupt Parliament and a
corrupting king.

Ministers were not all corrupt or place-hunters.
One of them, the Earl of Dartmouth, was a saint
in spirit. Lord North, the king's chief minister,

was not corrupt. He disliked his office and wished
to leave it.   In truth no sweeping simplicity of
condemnation will include all the ministers of
George III except on this one point that they
allowed to dictate their policy a narrow-minded
and ignorant king.   It was their right to furnish a
policy and to exercise the powers of government,
appoint to office, spend the public revenues.   Instead they let the King say that the opinions of his
ministers had no avail with him.   If we ask why,
the answer is that there was a mixture of motives.
North stayed in office because the King appealed
to his loyalty, a plea hard to resist under an ancient
monarchy.   Others stayed from love of power or
for what they could get.   In that golden age of
patronage it was possible for a man to hold a plural-
ity of offices which would bring to himself many
thousands of pounds a year, and also to secure the
reversion of offices and pensions to his children.
Horace Walpole spent a long life in luxurious ease
because of offices with high pay and few duties
secured in the distant days of his father's political
power.   Contracts to supply the army and the
navy went to friends of the government, sometimes
with disastrous results, since the contractor often
knew nothing of the business he undertook.   When,

in 1777, the Admiralty boasted that thirty-five ships of war were ready to put to sea it was found that there were in fact only six. The system nearly ruined the navy. It actually happened that planks of a man-of-war fell out through rot and that she sank. Often ropes and spars could not be had when most needed. When a public loan was floated the King's friends and they alone were given the shares at a price which enabled them to make large profits on the stock market.

The system could endure only as long as the King's friends had a majority in the House of Commons. Elections must be looked after. The King must have those on whom he could always depend. He controlled offices and pensions. With these things he bought members and he had to keep them bought by repeating the benefits. If the holder of a public office was thought to be dying the King was already naming to his Prime Minister the person to whom the office must go when death should occur. He insisted that many posts previously granted for life should now be given during his pleasure so that he might dismiss the holders at will. He watched the words and the votes in Parliament of public men and woe to those in his power if they displeased him. When he knew that

Fox, his great antagonist, would be absent from Parliament he pressed through measures which Fox would have opposed. It was not until George III was King that the buying and selling of boroughs became common. The King bought votes in the boroughs by paying high prices for trifles. He even went over the lists of voters and had names of servants of the government inserted if this seemed needed to make a majority secure. One of the most unedifying scenes in English history is that of George making a purchase in a shop at Windsor and because of this patronage asking for the shopkeeper's support in a local election. The King was saving and penurious in his habits that he might have the more money to buy votes. When he had no money left he would go to Parliament and ask for a special grant for his needs and the bought members could not refuse the money for their buying.

The people of England knew that Parliament was corrupt. But how to end the system? The press was not free. Some of it the government bought and the rest it tried to intimidate though often happily in vain. Only fragments of the debates in Parliament were published. Not until 1779 did the House of Commons admit the public to its galleries. No great political meetings were allowed until just before the American war and in any case the masses had no votes. The great land-owners had in their control a majority of the con-stituencies. There were scores of pocket boroughs in which their nominees were as certain of election as peers were of their seats in the House of Lords. The disease of England was deep-seated. A wise king could do much, but while George III survived — and his reign lasted sixty years — there was no hope of a wise king. A strong minister could im-pose his will on the King. But only time and cir-cumstance could evolve a strong minister. Time and circumstance at length produced the younger Pitt. But it needed the tragedy of two long wars — those against the colonies and revolutionary France — before the nation finally threw off the system which permitted the personal rule of George III and caused the disruption of the Empire. It may thus be said with some truth that George Washington was instrumental in the salvation of England.

The ministers of George III loved the sports, the rivalries, the ease, the remoteness of their rural magnificence. Perverse fashion kept them in Lon-don even in April and May for "the season," just

when in the country nature was most alluring.
Otherwise they were off to their estates whenever
they could get away from town.   The American
Revolution was not remotely affected by this habit.
With ministers long absent in the country important questions were postponed or forgotten.   The
crisis which in the end brought France into the
war was partly due to the carelessness of a minister
hurrying away to the country.   Lord George Germain, who directed military operations in America,
dictated a letter which would have caused General
Howe to move northward from New York to meet
General Burgoyne advancing from Canada.   Germain went off to the country without waiting to
sign the letter; it was mislaid among other papers;
Howe was without needed instructions; and the
disaster followed of Burgoyne's surrender.   Fox
pointed out, that, at a time when there was a
danger that a foreign army might land in England,
not one of the King's ministers was less than fifty
miles from London.   They were in their parks and
gardens, or hunting or fishing.   Nor did they stay
away for a few days only.   The absence was for
weeks or even months.

It is to the credit of Whig leaders in England,
landowners and aristocrats as they were, that they

supported with passion the American cause.   In
America, where the forces of the Revolution were
in control, the Loyalist who dared to be bold for
his opinions was likely to be tarred and feathered
and to lose his property.   There was an embittered
intolerance.   In England, however, it was an open
question in society whether to be for or against the
American cause.   The Duke of Richmond, a great
grandson of Charles II, said in the House of Lords
that under no code should the fighting Americans
be considered traitors.   What they did was "perfectly justifiable in every possible political and
moral sense."   All the world knows that Chatham and Burke and Fox urged the conciliation
of America and hundreds took the same stand.
Burke said of General Conway, a man of position,
that when he secured a majority in the House of
Commons against the Stamp Act his face shone as
the face of an angel.   Since the bishops almost to
a man voted with the King, Conway attacked them
as in this untrue to their high office.   Sir George
Savile, whose benevolence, supported by great
wealth, made him widely respected and loved, said
that the Americans were right in appealing to arms.
Coke of Norfolk was a landed magnate who lived
in regal style.   His seat of Holkham was one of

those great new palaces which the age reared at
such elaborate cost. It was full of beautiful things
— the art of Michelangelo, Raphael, Titian, and
Van Dyke, rare manuscripts, books, and tapestries.
So magnificent was Coke that a legend long ran
that his horses were shod with gold and that the
wheels of his chariots were of solid silver. In the
country he drove six horses. In town only the
King did this. Coke despised George III, chiefly
on account of his American policy, and to avoid the
reproach of rivaling the King's estate, he took joy
in driving past the palace in London with a donkey
as his sixth animal and in flicking his whip at the
King. When he was offered a peerage by the King
he denounced with fiery wrath the minister through
whom it was offered as attempting to bribe him.
Coke declared that if one of the King's ministers
held up a hat in the House of Commons and said
that it was a green bag the majority of the members
would solemnly vote that it was a green bag. The
bribery which brought this blind obedience of
Toryism filled Coke with fury. In youth he had
been taught never to trust a Tory and he could
say "I never have and, by God, I never will." One
of his children asked their mother whether Tories
were born wicked or after birth became wicked.

The uncompromising answer was: "They are born wicked and they grow up worse."

There is, of course, in much of this something of the malignance of party. In an age when one reverend theologian, Toplady, called another theologian, John Wesley, "a low and puny tadpole in Divinity" we must expect harsh epithets. But behind this bitterness lay a deep conviction of the righteousness of the American cause. At a great banquet at Holkham, Coke omitted the toast of the King; but every night during the American war he drank the health of Washington as the greatest man on earth. The war, he said, was the King's war, ministers were his tools, the press was bought. He denounced later the King's reception of the traitor Arnold. When the King's degenerate son, who became George IV, after some special misconduct, wrote to propose his annual visit to Holkham, Coke replied, "Holkham is open to *strangers* on Tuesdays." It was an independent and irate England which spoke in Coke. Those who paid taxes, he said, should control those who governed. America was not getting fair play. Both Coke and Fox, and no doubt many others, wore waistcoats of blue and buff because these were the colors of the uniforms of Washington's army.

Washington and Coke exchanged messages and they would have been congenial companions; for Coke, like Washington, was above all a farmer and tried to improve agriculture. Never for a moment, he said, had time hung heavy on his hands in the country. He began on his estate the culture of the potato, and for some time the best he could hear of it from his stolid tenantry was that it would not poison the pigs. Coke would have fought the levy of a penny of unjust taxation and he understood Washington. The American gentleman and the English gentleman had a common outlook.

Now had come, however, the hour for political separation. By reluctant but inevitable steps America made up its mind to declare for independence. At first continued loyalty to the King was urged on the plea that he was in the hands of evil-minded ministers, inspired by diabolical rage, or in those of an "infernal villain" such as the soldier, General Gage, a second Pharaoh; though it must be admitted that even then the King was "the tyrant of Great Britain." After Bunker Hill spasmodic declarations of independence were made here and there by local bodies. When Congress

organized an army, invaded Canada, and besieged
Boston, it was hard to protest loyalty to a King
whose forces were those of an enemy. Moreover
independence would, in the eyes at least of foreign
governments, give the colonies the rights of belligerents and enable them to claim for their fighting
forces the treatment due to a regular army and the
exchange of prisoners with the British. They could,
too, make alliances with other nations. Some
clamored for independence for a reason more sinister — that they might punish those who held to
the King and seize their property. There were
thirteen colonies in arms and each of them had to
form some kind of government which would work
without a king as part of its mechanism. One by
one such governments were formed. King George,
as we have seen, helped the colonies to make up
their minds. They were in no mood to be called
erring children who must implore undeserved
mercy and not force a loving parent to take un-
willing vengeance. "Our plantations" and "our
subjects in the colonies" would simply not learn
obedience. If George III would not reply to their
petitions until they laid down their arms, they
could manage to get on without a king. If England,
as Horace Walpole admitted, would not take them

seriously and speakers in Parliament called them obscure ruffians and cowards, so much the worse for England.

It was an Englishman, Thomas Paine, who fanned the fire into unquenchable flames. He had recently been dismissed from a post in the excise in England and was at this time earning in Philadelphia a precarious living by his pen. Paine said it was the interest of America to break the tie with Europe. Was a whole continent in America to be governed by an island a thousand leagues away? Of what advantage was it to remain connected with Great Britain? It was said that a united British Empire could defy the world, but why should America defy the world? "Everything that is right or natural pleads for separation." Interested men, weak men, prejudiced men, moderate men who do not really know Europe, may urge reconciliation, but nature is against it. Paine broke loose in that denunciation of kings with which ever since the world has been familiar. The wretched Briton, said Paine, is under a king and where there was a king there was no security for liberty. Kings were crowned ruffians and George III in particular was a sceptered savage, a royal brute, and other evil things. He had inflicted on America injuries not to be forgiven. The blood of the slain, not less than the true interests of posterity, demanded separation. Paine called his pamphlet *Common Sense*. It was published on January 9, 1776. More than a hundred thousand copies were quickly sold and it brought decision to many wavering minds.

In the first days of 1776 independence had become a burning question. New England had made up its mind. Virginia was keen for separation, keener even than New England. New York and Pennsylvania long hesitated and Maryland and North Carolina were very lukewarm. Early in 1776 Washington was advocating independence and Greene and other army leaders were of the same mind. Conservative forces delayed the settlement, and at last Virginia, in this as in so many other things taking the lead, instructed its delegates to urge a declaration by Congress of independence. Richard Henry Lee, a member of that honored family which later produced the ablest soldier of the Civil War, moved in Congress on June 7, 1776, that "these United Colonies are, and of right ought to be, Free and Independent States." The preparation of a formal declaration was referred to a committee of which John Adams and Thomas Jefferson were members. It is interesting to note that each of them became President of the United States and that both died on July 4, 1826, the fiftieth anniversary of the Declaration of Independence. Adams related long after that he and Jefferson formed the sub-committee to draft the Declaration and that he urged Jefferson to undertake the task since "you can write ten times better than I can." Jefferson accordingly wrote the paper. Adams was delighted "with its high tone and the flights of Oratory" but he did not approve of the flaming attack on the King, as a tyrant. "I never believed," he said, "George to be a tyrant in disposition and in nature." There was, he thought, too much passion for a grave and solemn document. He was, however, the principal speaker in its support.

There is passion in the Declaration from beginning to end, and not the restrained and chastened passion which we find in the great utterances of an American statesman of a later day, Abraham Lincoln. Compared with Lincoln, Jefferson is indeed a mere amateur in the use of words. Lincoln would not have scattered in his utterances overwrought phrases about "death, desolation and tyranny" or talked about pledging "our lives, our fortunes and our sacred honour." He indulged in no "Flights of Oratory." The passion in the Declaration is concentrated against the King. We do not know what were the emotions of George when he read it. We know that many Englishmen thought that it spoke truth. Exaggerations there are which make the Declaration less than a completely candid document. The King is accused of abolishing English laws in Canada with the intention of "introducing the same absolute rule into these colonies." What had been done in Canada was to let the conquered French retain their own laws — which was not tyranny but magnanimity. Another clause of the Declaration, as Jefferson first wrote it, made George responsible for the slave trade in America with all its horrors and crimes. We may doubt whether that not too enlightened monarch had even more than vaguely heard of the slave trade. This phase of the attack upon him was too much for the slave owners of the South and the slave traders of New England, and the clause was struck out.

Nearly fourscore and ten years later, Abraham Lincoln, at a supreme crisis in the nation's life, told in Independence Hall, Philadelphia, what the Declaration of Independence meant to him. "I have never," he said, "had a feeling politically

which did not spring from the sentiments in the
Declaration of Independence"; and then he spoke
of the sacrifices which the founders of the Republic
had made for these principles. He asked, too,
what was the idea which had held together the
nation thus founded. It was not the breaking
away from Great Britain. It was the assertion of
human right. We should speak in terms of reverence of a document which became a classic utterance of political right and which inspired Lincoln
in his fight to end slavery and to make "Liberty
and the pursuit of Happiness" realities for all men.
In England the colonists were often taunted with
being "rebels." The answer was not wanting that
ancestors of those who now cried "rebel" had
themselves been rebels a hundred years earlier
when their own liberty was at stake.

There were in Congress men who ventured to
say that the Declaration was a libel on the government of England; men like John Dickinson of
Pennsylvania and John Jay of New York, who
feared that the radical elements were moving too
fast. Radicalism, however, was in the saddle,
and on the 2d of July the "resolution respecting
independency" was adopted. On July 4, 1776,
Congress debated and finally adopted the formal

Declaration of Independence. The members did not vote individually. The delegates from each colony cast the vote of the colony. Twelve colonies voted for the Declaration. New York alone was silent because its delegates had not been instructed as to their vote, but New York, too, soon fell into line. It was a momentous occasion and was understood to be such. The vote seems to have been reached in the late afternoon. Anxious citizens were waiting in the streets. There was a bell in the State House, and an old ringer waited there for the signal. When there was long delay he is said to have muttered: "They will never do it! they will never do it!" Then came the word, "Ring! Ring!" It is an odd fact that the inscription on the bell, placed there long before the days of the trouble, was from Leviticus: "*Proclaim liberty throughout all the land unto all the inhabitants thereof.*" The bells of Philadelphia rang and cannon boomed. As the news spread there were bonfires and illuminations in all the colonies. On the day after the Declaration the Virginia Convention struck out "O Lord, save the King" from the church service. On the 10th of July Washington, who by this time had moved to New York, paraded the army and had the Declaration read at the head of each brigade.

That evening the statue of King George in New York was laid in the dust. It is a comment on the changes in human fortune that within little more than a year the British had taken Philadelphia, that the clamorous bell had been hid away for safety, and that colonial wiseacres were urging the rescinding of the ill-timed Declaration and the reunion of the British Empire.

CHAPTER IV

THE LOSS OF NEW YORK

WASHINGTON'S success at Boston had one good
effect. It destroyed Tory influence in that Puritan
stronghold. New England was henceforth of a
temper wholly revolutionary; and New England
tradition holds that what its people think today
other Americans think tomorrow. But, in the
summer of this year 1776, though no serious foe
was visible at any point in the revolted colonies, a
menace haunted every one of them. The British
had gone away by sea; by sea they would return.
On land armies move slowly and visibly; but on the
sea a great force may pass out of sight and then
suddenly reappear at an unexpected point. This
is the haunting terror of sea power. Already the
British had destroyed Falmouth, now Portland,
Maine, and Norfolk, the principal town in Virginia. Washington had no illusions of security.
He was anxious above all for the safety of New

York, commanding the vital artery of the Hudson, which must at all costs be defended. Accordingly, in April, he took his army to New York and established there his own headquarters.

Even before Washington moved to New York, three great British expeditions were nearing America. One of these we have already seen at Quebec. Another was bound for Charleston, to land there an army and to make the place a rallying center for the numerous but harassed Loyalists of the South. The third and largest of these expeditions was to strike at New York and, by a show of strength, bring the colonists to reason and reconciliation. If mildness failed the British intended to capture New York, sail up the Hudson and cut off New England from the other colonies.

The squadron destined for Charleston carried an army in command of a fine soldier, Lord Cornwallis, destined later to be the defeated leader in the last dramatic scene of the war. In May this fleet reached Wilmington, North Carolina, and took on board two thousand men under General Sir Henry Clinton, who had been sent by Howe from Boston in vain to win the Carolinas and who now assumed military command of the combined forces. Admiral Sir Peter Parker commanded the fleet. and

on the 4th of June he was off Charleston Harbor.
Parker found that in order to cross the bar he
would have to lighten his larger ships. This was
done by the laborious process of removing the guns,
which, of course, he had to replace when the bar
was crossed. On the 28th of June, Parker drew up
his ships before Fort Moultrie in the harbor. He
had expected simultaneous aid by land from three
thousand soldiers put ashore from the fleet on a
sandbar, but these troops could give him no help
against the fort from which they were cut off by a
channel of deep water. A battle soon proved the
British ships unable to withstand the American
fire from Fort Moultrie. Late in the evening Parker drew off, with two hundred and twenty-five
casualties against an American loss of thirty-seven.
The check was greater than that of Bunker Hill,
for there the British took the ground which they
attacked. The British sailors bore witness to the
gallantry of the defense: "We never had such a
drubbing in our lives," one of them testified.
Only one of Parker's ten ships was seaworthy after
the fight. It took him three weeks to refit, and not
until the 4th of August did his defeated ships reach
New York.

A mighty armada of seven hundred ships had

meanwhile sailed into the Bay of New York. This
fleet was commanded by Admiral Lord Howe and
it carried an army of thirty thousand men led by
his younger brother, Sir William Howe, who had
commanded at Bunker Hill. The General was an
able and well-informed soldier. He had a brilliant
record of service in the Seven Years' War, with
Wolfe in Canada, then in France itself, and in the
West Indies. In appearance he was tall, dark, and
coarse. His face showed him to be a free user of
wine. This may explain some of his faults as a
general. He trusted too much to subordinates; he
was leisurely and rather indolent, yet capable of
brilliant and rapid action. In America his heart
was never in his task. He was member of Parliament for Nottingham and had publicly condemned
the quarrel with America and told his electors that
in it he would take no command. He had not kept
his word, but his convictions remained. It would
be to accuse Howe of treason to say that he did not
do his best in America. Lack of conviction, however, affects action. Howe had no belief that his
country was in the right in the war and this handicapped him as against the passionate conviction of
Washington that all was at stake which made life
worth living.

The General's elder brother, Lord Howe, was another Whig who had no belief that the war was just. He sat in the House of Lords while his brother sat in the House of Commons. We rather wonder that the King should have been content to leave in Whig hands his fortunes in America both by land and sea. At any rate, here were the Howes more eager to make peace than to make war and commanded to offer terms of reconciliation. Lord Howe had an unpleasant face, so dark that he was called "Black Dick"; he was a silent, awkward man, shy and harsh in manner. In reality, however, he was kind, liberal in opinion, sober, and beloved by those who knew him best. His pacific temper towards America was not due to a dislike of war. He was a fighting sailor. Nearly twenty years later, on June 1, 1794, when he was in command of a fleet in touch with the French enemy, the sailors watched him to find any indication that the expected action would take place. Then the word went round: "We shall have the fight today; Black Dick has been smiling." They had it, and Howe won a victory which makes his name famous in the annals of the sea.

By the middle of July the two brothers were at New York. The soldier, having waited at Halifax since the evacuation of Boston, had arrived, and landed his army on Staten Island, on the day before Congress made the Declaration of Independence, which, as now we can see, ended finally any chance of reconciliation. The sailor arrived nine days later. Lord Howe was wont to regret that he had not arrived a little earlier, since the concessions which he had to offer might have averted the Declaration of Independence.   In truth, however, he had little to offer.   Humor and imagination are useful gifts in carrying on human affairs, but George III had neither.   He saw no lack of humor in now once more offering full and free pardon to a repentant Washington and his comrades, though John Adams was excepted by name[1]; in repudiating the right to exist of the Congress at Philadelphia, and in refusing to recognize the military rank of the rebel general whom it had named: he was to be addressed in civilian style as " George Washington Esq."   The King and his ministers had no imagination to call up the picture of high-hearted men fighting for rights which they held dear.

Lord Howe went so far as to address a letter to " George Washington Esq. &c. &c.," and Washington agreed to an interview with the officer who

[1] Trevelyan, *American Revolution*, Part ii, vol. i (New Ed., vol. ii). 261.

bore it. In imposing uniform and with the state-
liest manner, Washington, who had an instinct for
effect, received the envoy. The awed messenger
explained that the symbols " &c. &c." meant everything, including, of course, military titles; but
Washington only said smilingly that they might
mean anything, including, of course, an insult, and
refused to take the letter. He referred to Congress,
a body which Howe could not recognize, the grave
question of the address on an envelope and Congress agreed that the recognition of his rank was
necessary. There was nothing to do but to go on
with the fight.

Washington's army held the city of New York,
at the southerly point of Manhattan Island. The
Hudson River, separating the island from the mainland of New Jersey on the west, is at its mouth
two miles wide. The northern and eastern sides of
the island are washed by the Harlem River, flowing
out of the Hudson about a dozen miles north of the
city, and broadening into the East River, about
a mile wide where it separates New York from
Brooklyn Heights, on Long Island. Encamped on
Staten Island, on the south, General Howe could,
with the aid of the fleet, land at any of half a
dozen vulnerable points. Howe had the further

advantage of a much larger force.   Washington had in all some twenty thousand men, numbers of them serving for short terms and therefore for the most part badly drilled.   Howe had twenty-five thousand well-trained soldiers, and he could, in addition, draw men from the fleet, which would give him in all double the force of Washington.

In such a situation even the best skill of Washington was likely only to qualify defeat.   He was advised to destroy New York and retire to positions more tenable.   But even if he had so desired, Congress, his master, would not permit him to burn the city, and he had to make plans to defend it.   Brooklyn Heights so commanded New York that enemy cannon planted there would make the city untenable.   Accordingly Washington placed half his force on Long Island to defend Brooklyn Heights and in doing so made the fundamental error of cutting his army in two and dividing it by an arm of the sea in presence of overwhelming hostile naval power.

On the 22d of August Howe ferried fifteen thousand men across the Narrows to Long Island, in order to attack the position on Brooklyn Heights from the rear.   Before him lay wooded hills across which led three roads converging at Brooklyn

Heights beyond the hills. On the east a fourth road led round the hills. In the dark of the night of the 26th of August Howe set his army in motion on all these roads, in order by daybreak to come to close quarters with the Americans and drive them back to the Heights. The movement succeeded perfectly. The British made terrible use of the bayonet. By the evening of the twenty-seventh the Americans, who fought well against overwhelming odds, had lost nearly two thousand men in casualties and prisoners, six field pieces, and twenty-six heavy guns. The two chief commanders, Sullivan and Stirling, were among the prisoners, and what was left of the army had been driven back to Brooklyn Heights. Howe's critics said that had he pressed the attack further he could have made certain the capture of the whole American force on Long Island.

Criticism of what might have been is easy and usually futile. It might be said of Washington, too, that he should not have kept an army so far in front of his lines behind Brooklyn Heights facing a superior enemy, and with, for a part of it, retreat possible only by a single causeway across a marsh three miles long. When he realized, on the 28th of August, what Howe had achieved, he increased the

defenders of Brooklyn Heights to ten thousand
men, more than half his army. This was another
cardinal error. British ships were near and but
for unfavorable winds might have sailed up to
Brooklyn. Washington hoped and prayed that
Howe would try to carry Brooklyn Heights by
assault. Then there would have been at least
slaughter on the scale of Bunker Hill. But Howe
had learned caution. He made no reckless attack,
and soon Washington found that he must move
away or face the danger of losing every man on
Long Island.

On the night of the 29th of August there was
clear moonlight, with fog towards daybreak. A
British army of twenty-five thousand men was
only some six hundred yards from the American
lines. A few miles from the shore lay at anchor a
great British fleet with, it is to be presumed, its
patrols on the alert. Yet, during that night, ten
thousand American troops were marched down to
boats on the strand at Brooklyn and, with all their
stores, were carried across a mile of water to New
York. There must have been the splash of oars
and the grating of keels, orders given in tones
above a whisper, the complex sounds of moving
bodies of men. It was all done under the eye of

Washington. We can picture that tall figure
moving about on the strand at Brooklyn, which
he was the last to leave. Not a sound disturbed
the slumbers of the British. An army in retreat
does not easily defend itself. Boats from the British fleet might have brought panic to the Americans in the darkness and the British army should
at least have known that they were gone. By
seven in the morning the ten thousand American
soldiers were for the time safe in New York, and
we may suppose that the two Howes were asking eager questions and wondering how it had
all happened.

Washington had shown that he knew when and
how to retire. Long Island was his first battle and
he had lost. Now retreat was his first great tactical
achievement. He could not stay in New York and
so sent at once the chief part of the army, with-
drawn from Brooklyn, to the line of the Harlem
River at the north end of the island. He realized
that his shore batteries could not keep the British
fleet from sailing up both the East and the Hudson
Rivers and from landing a force on Manhattan
Island almost where it liked. Then the city of New
York would be surrounded by a hostile fleet and a
hostile army. The Howes could have performed

this maneuver as soon as they had a favor-able wind. There was, we know, great confusion in New York, and Washington tells us how his heart was torn by the distress of the inhabitants. The British gave him plenty of time to make plans, and for a reason. We have seen that Lord Howe was not only an admiral to make war but also an envoy to make peace. The British victory on Long Island might, he thought, make Congress more willing to negotiate. So now he sent to Philadel-phia the captured American General Sullivan, with the request that some members of Congress might confer privately on the prospects for peace.

Howe probably did not realize that the Ameri-cans had the British quality of becoming more resolute by temporary reverses. By this time, too, suspicion of every movement on the part of Great Britain had become a mania. Every one in Con-gress seems to have thought that Howe was plan-ning treachery. John Adams, excepted by name from British offers of pardon, called Sullivan a "decoy duck" and, as he confessed, laughed, scolded, and grieved at any negotiation. The wish to talk privately with members of Congress was called an insulting way of avoiding recognition of that body. In spite of this, even the stalwart

Adams and the suave Franklin were willing to be members of a committee which went to meet Lord Howe. With great sorrow Howe now realized that he had no power to grant what Congress insisted upon,. the recognition of independence, as a preliminary to negotiation. There was nothing for it but war.

On the 15th of September the British struck the blow too long delayed had war been their only interest. New York had to sit nearly helpless while great men-of-war passed up both the Hudson and the East River with guns sweeping the shores of Manhattan Island. At the same time General Howe sent over in boats from Long Island to the landing at Kip's Bay, near the line of the present Thirty-fourth Street, an army to cut off the city from the northern part of the island. Washington marched in person with two New England regiments to dispute the landing and give him time for evacuation. To his rage panic seized his men and they turned and fled, leaving him almost alone not a hundred yards from the enemy. A stray shot at that moment might have influenced greatly modern history, for, as events were soon to show, Washington was the mainstay of the American cause. He too had to get away and Howe's force landed easily enough.

Meanwhile, on the west shore of the island, there was an animated scene. The roads were crowded with refugees fleeing northward from New York. These civilians Howe had no reason to stop, but there marched, too, out of New York four thousand men, under Israel Putnam, who got safely away northward. Only leisurely did Howe extend his line across the island so as to cut off the city. The story, not more trustworthy than many other legends of war, is that Mrs. Murray, living in a country house near what now is Murray Hill, invited the General to luncheon, and that to enjoy this pleasure he ordered a halt for his whole force. Generals sometimes do foolish things but it is not easy to call up a picture of Howe, in the midst of a busy movement of troops, receiving the lady's invitation, accepting it, and ordering the whole army to halt while he lingered over the luncheon table. There is no doubt that his mind was still divided between making war and making peace. Probably Putnam had already got away his men, and there was no purpose in stopping the refugees in that flight from New York which so aroused the pity of Washington. As it was Howe took sixty-seven guns. By accident, or, it is said, by design of the Americans themselves, New York soon took fire and one-third of the little city was burned.

After the fall of New York there followed a complex campaign. The resourceful Washington was now, during his first days of active warfare, pitting himself against one of the most experienced of British generals. Fleet and army were acting together. The aim of Howe was to get control of the Hudson and to meet half way the advance from Canada by way of Lake Champlain which Carleton was leading. On the 12th of October, when autumn winds were already making the nights cold, Howe moved. He did not attack Washington who lay in strength at the Harlem. That would have been to play Washington's game. Instead he put the part of his army still on Long Island in ships which then sailed through the dangerous currents of Hell Gate and landed at Throg's Neck, a peninsula on the sound across from Long Island. Washington parried this movement by so guarding the narrow neck of the peninsula leading to the mainland that the cautious Howe shrank from a frontal attack across a marsh. After a delay of six days, he again embarked his army, landed a few miles above Throg's Neck in the hope of cutting off Washington from retreat northward, only to find

Washington still north of him at White Plains. A sharp skirmish followed in which Howe lost over two hundred men and Washington only one hundred and forty. Washington, masterly in retreat, then withdrew still farther north among hills difficult of attack.

Howe had a plan which made a direct attack on Washington unnecessary. He turned southward and occupied the east shore of the Hudson River. On the 16th of November took place the worst disaster which had yet befallen American arms. Fort Washington, lying just south of the Harlem, was the only point still held on Manhattan Island by the Americans. In modern war it has become clear that fortresses supposedly strong may be only traps for their defenders. Fort Washington stood on the east bank of the Hudson opposite Fort Lee, on the west bank. These forts could not fulfil the purpose for which they were intended, of stopping British ships. Washington saw that the two forts should be abandoned. But the civilians in Congress, who, it must be remembered, named the generals and had final authority in directing the war, were reluctant to accept the loss involved in abandoning the forts and gave orders that every effort should be made to hold them. Greene, on the whole Washington's best general, was in command of the two positions and was left to use his own judgment. On the 15th of November, by a sudden and rapid march across the island, Howe appeared before Fort Washington and summoned it to surrender on pain of the rigors of war, which meant putting the garrison to the sword should he have to take the place by storm.   The answer was a defiance; and on the next day Howe attacked in overwhelming force.   There was severe fighting. The casualties of the British were nearly five hundred, but they took the huge fort with its three thousand defenders and a great quantity of munitions of war. Howe's threat was not carried out. There was no massacre.

Across the river at Fort Lee the helpless Washington watched this great disaster. He had need still to look out, for Fort Lee was itself doomed. On the nineteenth Lord Cornwallis with five thousand men crossed the river five miles above Fort Lee.   General Greene barely escaped with the two thousand men in the fort, leaving behind one hundred and forty cannon, stores, tools, and even the men's blankets.   On the twentieth the British flag was floating over Fort Lee and Washington's whole force was in rapid flight across New Jersey, hardly pausing until it had been ferried over the Delaware River into Pennsylvania.

Treachery, now linked to military disaster, made Washington's position terrible.   Charles Lee, Horatio Gates, and Richard Montgomery were three important officers of the regular British army who fought on the American side.   Montgomery had been killed at Quebec; the defects of Gates were not yet conspicuous; and Lee was next to Washington the most trusted American general. The names Washington and Lee of the twin forts on opposite sides of the Hudson show how the two generals stood in the public mind.   While disaster was overtaking Washington, Lee had seven thousand men at North Castle on the east bank of the Hudson, a few miles above Fort Washington, blocking Howe's advance farther up the river.   On the day after the fall of Fort Washington, Lee received positive orders to cross the Hudson at once. Three days later Fort Lee fell, and Washington repeated the order.   Lee did not budge.   He was safe where he was and could cross the river and get away into New Jersey when he liked.   He seems deliberately to have left Washington to face complete disaster and thus prove his incompetence; then, as the undefeated general, he could take the chief command. There is no evidence that he had intrigued with Howe, but he thought that he could be the peacemaker between Great Britain and America, with untold possibilities of ambition in that rôle. He wrote of Washington at this time, to his friend Gates, as weak and "most damnably deficient." Nemesis, however, overtook him. In the end he had to retreat across the Hudson to northern New Jersey. Here many of the people were Tories. Lee fell into a trap, was captured in bed at a tavern by a hard-riding party of British cavalry, and carried off a prisoner, obliged to bestride a horse in night gown and slippers. Not always does fate appear so just in her strokes.

In December, though the position of Washington was very bad, all was not lost. The chief aim of Howe was to secure the line of the Hudson and this he had not achieved. At Stony Point, which lies up the Hudson about fifty miles from New York, the river narrows and passes through what is almost a mountain gorge, easily defended. Here Washington had erected fortifications which made it at least difficult for a British force to pass up the river. Moreover in the highlands of northern New Jersey, with headquarters at Morristown, General Sullivan, recently exchanged, and General Gates now had Lee's army and also the remnants of the force driven from Canada. But in retreating across New Jersey Washington had been forsaken by thousands of men, beguiled in part by the Tory population, discouraged by defeat, and in many cases with the right to go home, since their term of service had expired. All that remained of Washington's army after the forces of Sullivan and Gates joined him across the Delaware in Pennsylvania, was about four thousand men.

Howe was determined to have Philadelphia as well as New York and could place some reliance on Tory help in Pennsylvania. He had pursued Washington to the Delaware and would have pushed on across that river had not his alert foe taken care that all the boats should be on the wrong shore. As it was, Howe occupied the left bank of the Delaware with his chief post at Trenton. If he made sure of New Jersey he could go on to Philadelphia when the river was frozen over or indeed when he liked. Even the Congress had fled to Baltimore. There were British successes in other quarters. Early in December Lord Howe took the fleet to Newport. Soon he controlled the whole of Rhode Island and checked the American privateers who had made it their base. The brothers issued proclamations offering protection to all who should within sixty days return to their British allegiance and many people of high standing in New York and New Jersey accepted the offer. Howe wrote home to England the glad news of victory. Philadelphia would probably fall before spring and it looked as if the war was really over.

In this darkest hour Washington struck a blow which changed the whole situation. We associate with him the thought of calm deliberation. Now, however, was he to show his strongest quality as a general to be audacity. At the Battle of the Marne, in 1914, the French General Foch sent the despatch: "My center is giving way; my right is retreating; the situation is excellent: I am attacking." Washington's position seemed as nearly hopeless and he, too, had need of some striking action. A campaign marked by his own blundering and by the treachery of a trusted general had ended in seeming ruin. Pennsylvania at his back and New Jersey before him across the Delaware were less than half loyal to the American cause and probably willing to accept peace on almost any terms. Never was a general in a position where greater risks must be taken for salvation. As Washington pondered what was going on among the British

across the Delaware, a bold plan outlined itself in
his mind. Howe, he knew, had gone to New York
to celebrate a triumphant Christmas. His absence
from the front was certain to involve slackness.
It was Germans who held the line of the Delaware,
some thirteen hundred of them under Colonel
Rahl at Trenton, two thousand under Von Donop
farther down the river at Bordentown; and with
Germans perhaps more than any other people
Christmas is a season of elaborate festivity. On
this their first Christmas away from home many of
the Germans would be likely to be off their guard
either through homesickness or dissipation. They
cared nothing for either side. There had been
much plundering in New Jersey and discipline
was relaxed.

Howe had been guilty of the folly of making
strong the posts farthest from the enemy and weak
those nearest to him. He had, indeed, ordered
Rahl to throw up redoubts for the defense of Trenton, but this, as Washington well knew, had not
been done for Rahl despised his enemy and spoke
of the American army as already lost. Washington's bold plan was to recross the Delaware and
attack Trenton. There were to be three crossings.
One was to be against Von Donop at Bordentown

below Trenton, the second at Trenton itself. These two attacks were designed to prevent aid to Trenton. The third force with which Washington himself went was to cross the river some nine miles above the town.

Christmas Day, 1776, was dismally cold. There was a driving storm of sleet and the broad swollen stream of the Delaware, dotted with dark masses of floating ice, offered a chill prospect. To take an army with its guns across that threatening flood was indeed perilous. Gates and other generals declared that the scheme was too difficult to be carried out. Only one of the three forces crossed the river. Washington, with iron will, was not to be turned from his purpose. He had skilled boatmen from New England. The crossing took no less than ten hours and a great part of it was done in wintry darkness. When the army landed on the New Jersey shore it had a march of nine miles in sleet and rain in order to reach Trenton by daybreak. It is said that some of the men marched barefoot leaving tracks of blood in the snow. The arms of some were lost and those of others were wet and useless but Washington told them that they must depend the more on the bayonet. He attacked Trenton in broad daylight. There was a sharp fight.

Rahl, the commander, and some seventy men, were killed and a thousand men surrendered.

Even now Washington's position was dangerous. Von Donop, with two thousand men, lay only a few miles down the river. Had he marched at once on Trenton, as he should have done, the worn out little force of Washington might have met with disaster. What Von Donop did when the alarm reached him was to retreat as fast as he could to Princeton, a dozen miles to the rear towards New York, leaving behind his sick and all his heavy equipment. Meanwhile Washington, knowing his danger, had turned back across the Delaware with a prisoner for every two of his men. When, however, he saw what Von Donop had done he returned on the twenty-ninth to Trenton, sent out scouting parties, and roused the country so that in every bit of forest along the road to Princeton there were men, dead shots, to make difficult a British advance to retake Trenton.

The reverse had brought consternation at New York. Lord Cornwallis was about to embark for England, the bearer of news of overwhelming victory. Now, instead, he was sent to drive back Washington. It was no easy task for Cornwallis to reach Trenton, for Washington's scouting parties and a force of six hundred men under Greene were on the road to harass him. On the evening of the 2d of January, however, he reoccupied Trenton. This time Washington had not recrossed the Delaware but had retreated southward and was now entrenched on the southern bank of the little river Assanpink, which flows into the Delaware. Reinforcements were following Cornwallis. That night he sharply cannonaded Washington's position and was as sharply answered. He intended to attack in force in the morning. To the skill and resource of Washington he paid the compliment of saying that at last he had run down the "Old Fox."

Then followed a maneuver which, years after, Cornwallis, a generous foe, told Washington was one of the most surprising and brilliant in the history of war. There was another "old fox" in Europe, Frederick the Great, of Prussia, who knew war if ever man knew it, and he, too, from this movement ranked Washington among the great generals. The maneuver was simple enough. Instead of taking the obvious course of again retreating across the Delaware Washington decided to advance, to get in behind Cornwallis, to try to cut his communications, to threaten the British base of supply and then, if a superior force came up, to retreat into the highlands of New Jersey. There he could keep an unbroken line as far east as the Hudson, menace the British in New Jersey, and probably force them to withdraw to the safety of New York.

All through the night of January 2, 1777, Washington's camp fires burned brightly and the British outposts could hear the sound of voices and of the spade and pickaxe busy in throwing up entrenchments. The fires died down towards morning and the British awoke to find the enemy camp deserted. Washington had carried his whole army by a roundabout route to the Princeton road and now stood between Cornwallis and his base. There was some sharp fighting that day near Princeton. Washington had to defeat and get past the reinforcements coming to Cornwallis. He reached Princeton and then slipped away northward and made his headquarters at Morristown. He had achieved his purpose. The British with Washington entrenched on their flank were not safe in New Jersey. The only thing to do was to withdraw to New York. By his brilliant advance Washington recovered the whole of New Jersey with the exception of some minor positions near the sea. He had changed the face of the war. In London there was momentary rejoicing over Howe's recent victories, but it was soon followed by distressing news of defeat. Through all the colonies ran inspiring tidings. There had been doubts whether, after all, Washington was the heaven-sent leader. Now both America and Europe learned to recognize his skill. He had won a reputation, though not yet had he saved a cause.

CHAPTER V

THOUGH the outlook for Washington was brightened by his success in New Jersey, it was still depressing enough. The British had taken New York, they could probably take Philadelphia when they liked, and no place near the seacoast was safe. According to the votes in Parliament, by the spring of 1777 Britain was to have an army of eighty-nine thousand men, of whom fifty-seven thousand were intended for colonial garrisons and for the prosecution of the war in America. These numbers were in fact never reached, but the army of forty thousand in America was formidable compared with Washington's forces. The British were not hampered by the practice of enlisting men for only a few months, which marred so much of Washington's effort. Above all they had money and adequate resources. In a word they had the things which Washington lacked during almost the whole of the war.

108

Washington called his success in the attack at Trenton a lucky stroke. It was luck which had far-reaching consequences. Howe had the fixed idea that to follow the capture of New York by that of Philadelphia, the most populous city in America, and the seat of Congress, would mean great glory for himself and a crushing blow to the American cause. If to this could be added, as he intended, the occupation of the whole valley of the Hudson, the year 1777 might well see the end of the war. An acute sense of the value of time is vital in war. Promptness, the quick surprise of the enemy, was perhaps the chief military virtue of Washington; dilatoriness was the destructive vice of Howe. He had so little contempt for his foe that he practised a blighting caution. On April 12, 1777, Washington, in view of his own depleted force, in a state of half famine, wrote: "If Howe does not take advantage of our weak state he is very unfit for his trust." Howe remained inactive and time, thus despised, worked its due revenge. Later Howe did move, and with skill, but he missed the rapid combination in action which was the first condition of final success. He could have captured Philadelphia in May. He took the city, but not until September, when to hold it had become a liability and not an asset. To go there at all was perhaps unwise; to go in September was for him a tragic mistake.

From New York to Philadelphia the distance by land is about a hundred miles. The route lay across New Jersey, that "garden of America" which English travelers spoke of as resembling their own highly cultivated land. Washington had his headquarters at Morristown, in northern New Jersey. His resources were at a low ebb. He had always the faith that a cause founded on justice could not fail; but his letters at this time are full of depressing anxiety. Each State regarded itself as in danger and made care of its own interests its chief concern. By this time Congress had lost most of the able men who had given it dignity and authority. Like Howe it had slight sense of the value of time and imagined that tomorrow was as good as today. Wellington once complained that, though in supreme command, he had not authority to appoint even a corporal. Washington was hampered both by Congress and by the State Governments in choosing leaders. He had some officers, such as Greene, Knox, and Benedict Arnold, whom he trusted. Others, like Gates and Conway, were ceaseless intriguers. To General Sullivan, who fancied himself constantly slighted and ill-treated, Washington wrote sharply to abolish his poisonous suspicions.

Howe had offered easy terms to those in New Jersey who should declare their loyalty and to meet this Washington advised the stern policy of outlawing every one who would not take the oath of allegiance to the United States. There was much fluttering of heart on the New Jersey farms, much anxious trimming in order, in any event, to be safe. Howe's Hessians had plundered ruthlessly causing deep resentment against the British. Now Washington found his own people doing the same thing. Militia officers, themselves, "generally" as he said, "of the lowest class of the people," not only stole but incited their men to steal. It was easy to plunder under the plea that the owner of the property was a Tory, whether open or concealed, and Washington wrote that the waste and theft were "beyond all conception." There were shirkers claiming exemption from military service on the ground that they were doing necessary service as civilians. Washington needed maps to plan his intricate movements and could not get them. Smallpox was devastating his army and causing losses heavier than those from the enemy. When pay day came there was usually no money.

It is little wonder that in this spring of 1777 he feared that his army might suddenly dissolve and leave him without a command. In that case he would not have yielded. Rather, so stern and bitter was he against England, would he have plunged into the western wilderness to be lost in its vast spaces.

Howe had his own perplexities. He knew that a great expedition under Burgoyne was to advance from Canada southward to the Hudson. Was he to remain with his whole force at New York until the time should come to push up the river to meet Burgoyne? He had a copy of the instructions given in England to Burgoyne by Lord George Germain, but he was himself without orders. Afterwards the reason became known. Lord George Germain had dictated the order to coöperate with Burgoyne, but had hurried off to the country before it was ready for his signature and it had been mislaid. Howe seemed free to make his own plans and he longed to be master of the enemy's capital. In the end he decided to take Philadelphia — a task easy enough, as the event proved. At Howe's elbow was the traitorous American general, Charles Lee, whom he had recently captured, and Lee, as we know, told him

that Maryland and Pennsylvania were at heart
loyal to the King and panting to be free from the
tyranny of the demagogue.   Once firmly in the
capital Howe believed that he would have secure
control of Maryland, Pennsylvania, and New
Jersey.   He could achieve this and be back at New
York in time to meet Burgoyne, perhaps at Albany.
Then he would hold the colony of New York from
Staten Island to the Canadian frontier.   Howe
found that he could send ships up the Hudson, and
the American army had to stand on the banks
almost helpless against the mobility of sea power.
Washington's left wing rested on the Hudson and
he held both banks but neither at Peekskill nor, as
yet, farther up at West Point, could his forts prevent the passage of ships.   It was a different matter
for the British to advance on land.   But the ships
went up and down in the spring of 1777.   It would
be easy enough to help Burgoyne when the time
should come.

It was summer before Howe was ready to move,
and by that time he had received instructions that
his first aim must be to coöperate with Burgoyne.
First, however, he was resolved to have Philadelphia.   Washington watched Howe in perplexity.
A great fleet and a great army lay at New York.

8

Why did they not move? Washington knew perfectly well what he himself would have done in Howe's place. He would have attacked rapidly in April the weak American army and, after destroying or dispersing it, would have turned to meet Burgoyne coming southward from Canada. Howe did send a strong force into New Jersey. But he did not know how weak Washington really was, for that master of craft in war disseminated with great skill false information as to his own supposed overwhelming strength. Howe had been bitten once by advancing too far into New Jersey and was not going to take risks. He tried to entice Washington from the hills to attack in open country. He marched here and there in New Jersey and kept Washington alarmed and exhausted by counter marches, and always puzzled as to what the next move should be. Howe purposely let one of his secret messengers be taken bearing a despatch saying that the fleet was about to sail for Boston. All these things took time and the summer was slipping away. In the end Washington realized that Howe intended to make his move not by land but by sea. Could it be possible that he was not going to make aid to Burgoyne his chief purpose? Could it be that he would attack Boston? Washington

hoped so for he knew the reception certain at
Boston.   Or was his goal Charleston?   On the 23d
of July, when the summer was more than half
gone, Washington began to see more clearly.   On
that day Howe had embarked eighteen thousand
men and the fleet put to sea from Staten Island.

Howe was doing what able officers with him,
such as Cornwallis, Grey, and the German Knyphausen, appear to have been unanimous in thinking
he should not do.   He was misled not only by the
desire to strike at the very center of the rebellion,
but also by the assurance of the traitorous Lee that
to take Philadelphia would be the effective signal
to all the American Loyalists, the overwhelming
majority of the people, as was believed, that sedi-
tion had failed.   A tender parent, the King, was
ready to have the colonies back in their former
relation and to give them secure guarantees of
future liberty.   Any one who saw the fleet put out
from New York Harbor must have been impressed
with the might of Britain.   No less than two hundred and twenty-nine ships set their sails and
covered the sea for miles.   When they had disappeared out of sight of the New Jersey shore
their goal was still unknown.   At sea they might
turn in any direction.   Washington's uncertainty

was partly relieved on the 30th of July when the fleet appeared at the entrance of Delaware Bay, with Philadelphia some hundred miles away across the bay and up the Delaware River. After hovering about the Cape for a day the fleet again put to sea, and Washington, who had marched his army so as to be near Philadelphia, thought the whole movement a feint and knew not where the fleet would next appear. He was preparing to march to New York to menace General Clinton, who had there seven thousand men able to help Burgoyne when he heard good news. On the 22d of August he knew that Howe had really gone southward and was in Chesapeake Bay. Boston was now certainly safe. On the 25th of August, after three stormy weeks at sea, Howe arrived at Elkton, at the head of Chesapeake Bay, and there landed his army. It was Philadelphia fifty miles away that he intended to have. Washington wrote gleefully: "Now let all New England turn out and crush Burgoyne." Before the end of September he was writing that he was certain of complete disaster to Burgoyne.

Howe had, in truth, made a ruinous mistake. Had the date been May instead of August he might still have saved Burgoyne. But at the end of

August, when the net was closing on Burgoyne, Howe was three hundred miles away. His disregard of time and distance had been magnificent. In July he had sailed to the mouth of the Delaware, with Philadelphia near, but he had then sailed away again, and why? Because the passage of his ships up the river to the city was blocked by obstructions commanded by bristling forts. The naval officers said truly that the fleet could not get up the river. But Howe might have landed his army at the head of Delaware Bay. It is a dozen miles across the narrow peninsula from the head of Delaware Bay to that of Chesapeake Bay. Since Howe had decided to attack from the head of Chesapeake Bay there was little to prevent him from landing his army on the Delaware side of the peninsula and marching across it. By sea it is a voyage of three hundred miles round a peninsula one hundred and fifty miles long to get from one of these points to the other, by land only a dozen miles away. Howe made the sea voyage and spent on it three weeks when a march of a day would have saved this time and kept his fleet three hundred miles by sea nearer to New York and aid for Burgoyne.

Howe's mistakes only have their place in the procession to inevitable disaster. Once in the thick of fighting he showed himself formidable. When he had landed at Elkton he was fifty miles southwest of Philadelphia and between him and that place was Washington with his army. Washington was determined to delay Howe in every possible way. To get to Philadelphia Howe had to cross the Brandywine River. Time was nothing to him, He landed at Elkton on the 25th of August. Not until the 10th of September was he prepared to attack Washington barring his way at Chadd's Ford. Washington was in a strong position on a front of two miles on the river. At his left, below Chadd's Ford, the Brandywine is a torrent flowing between high cliffs. There the British would find no passage. On his right was a forest. Washington had chosen his position with his usual skill. Entrenchments protected his front and batteries would sweep down an advancing enemy. He had probably not more than eleven thousand men in the fight and it is doubtful whether Howe brought up a greater number so that the armies were not unevenly matched. At daybreak on the eleventh the British army broke camp at the village of Kenneth Square, four miles from Chadd's Ford, and, under General Knyphausen, marched straight to make a frontal attack on Washington's position.

In the battle which followed Washington was
beaten by the superior tactics of his enemy. Not
all of the British army was there in the attack at
Chadd's Ford. A column under Cornwallis had filed
off by a road to the left and was making a long and
rapid march. The plan was to cross the Brandywine some ten miles above where Washington was
posted and to attack him in the rear. By two
o'clock in the afternoon Cornwallis had forced the
two branches of the upper Brandywine and was
marching on Dilworth at the right rear of the
American army. Only then did Washington become aware of his danger. His first impulse was to
advance across Chadd's Ford to try to overwhelm
Knyphausen and thus to get between Howe and
the fleet at Elkton. This might, however, have
brought disaster and he soon decided to retire.
His movement was ably carried out. Both sides
suffered in the woodland fighting but that night
the British army encamped in Washington's position at Chadd's Ford, and Howe had fought
skillfully and won an important battle.

Washington had retired in good order and was
still formidable. He now realized clearly enough
that Philadelphia would fall. Delay, however,
would be nearly as good as victory. He saw what

Howe could not see, that menacing cloud in the
north, much bigger than a man's hand, which, with
Howe far away, should break in a final storm
terrible for the British cause. Meanwhile Washington meant to keep Howe occupied. Rain alone
prevented another battle before the British reached
the Schuylkill River. On that river Washington
guarded every ford. But, in the end, by skillful
maneuvering, Howe was able to cross and on the
26th of September he occupied Philadelphia without resistance. The people were ordered to remain
quietly in their houses. Officers were billeted on
the wealthier inhabitants. The fall resounded far
of what Lord Adam Gordon called a "great and
noble city," "the first Town in America," "one of
the Wonders of the World." Its luxury had been
so conspicuous that the austere John Adams condemned the "sinful feasts" in which he shared.
About it were fine country seats surrounded by
parklike grounds, with noble trees, clipped hedges,
and beautiful gardens. The British believed that
Pennsylvania was really on their side. Many of
the people were friendly and hundreds now renewed their oath of allegiance to the King. Washington complained that the people gave Howe information denied to him. They certainly fed

Howe's army willingly and received good British gold while Washington had only paper money with which to pay. Over the proud capital floated once more the British flag and people who did not see very far said that, with both New York and Philadelphia taken, the rebellion had at last collapsed.

Once in possession of Philadelphia Howe made his camp at Germantown, a straggling suburban village, about seven miles northwest of the city. Washington's army lay at the foot of some hills a dozen miles farther away. Howe had need to be wary, for Washington was the same "old fox" who had played so cunning a game at Trenton. The efforts of the British army were now centered on clearing the river Delaware so that supplies might be brought up rapidly by water instead of being carried fifty miles overland from Chesapeake Bay. Howe detached some thousands of men for this work and there was sharp fighting before the troops and the fleet combined had cleared the river. At Germantown Howe kept about nine thousand men. Though he knew that Washington was likely to attack him he did not entrench his army as he desired the attack to be made. It might well have succeeded. Washington with eleven thousand men aimed at a surprise. On the evening of the 3d of

October he set out from his camp. Four roads led into Germantown and all these the Americans used. At sunrise on the fourth, just as the attack began, a fog arose to embarrass both sides. Lying a little north of the village was the solid stone house of Chief Justice Chew, and it remains famous as the central point in the bitter fight of that day. What brought final failure to the American attack was an accident of maneuvering. Sullivan's brigade was in front attacking the British when Greene's came up for the same purpose. His line overlapped Sullivan's and he mistook in the fog Sullivan's men for the enemy and fired on them from the rear. A panic naturally resulted among the men who were attacked also at the same time by the British on their front. The disorder spread. British reinforcements arrived, and Washington drew off his army in surprising order considering the panic. He had six hundred and seventy-three casualties and lost besides four hundred prisoners. The British loss was five hundred and thirty-seven casualties and fourteen prisoners. The attack had failed, but news soon came which made the reverse unimportant. Burgoyne and his whole army had surrendered at Saratoga.

CHAPTER VI

THE FIRST GREAT BRITISH DISASTER

JOHN BURGOYNE, in a measure a soldier of fortune,
was the younger son of an impoverished baronet,
but he had married the daughter of the powerful
Earl of Derby and was well known in London
society as a man of fashion and also as a man of
letters, whose plays had a certain vogue. His will,
in which he describes himself as a humble Christian, who, in spite of many faults, had never forgotten God, shows that he was serious minded.
He sat in the House of Commons for Preston and,
though he used the language of a courtier and
spoke of himself as lying at the King's feet to await
his commands, he was a Whig, the friend of Fox
and others whom the King regarded as his enemies.
One of his plays describes the difficulties of getting
the English to join the army of George III. We have
the smartly dressed recruit as a decoy to suggest an
easy life in the army. Victory and glory are so

certain that a tailor stands with his feet on the neck of the King of France. The decks of captured ships swim with punch and are clotted with gold dust, and happy soldiers play with diamonds as if they were marbles. The senators of England, says Burgoyne, care chiefly to make sure of good game laws for their own pleasure. The worthless son of one of them, who sets out on the long drive to his father's seat in the country, spends an hour in "yawning, picking his teeth and damning his journey" and when once on the way drives with such fury that the route is marked by "yelping dogs, broken-backed pigs and dismembered geese."

It was under this playwright and satirist, who had some skill as a soldier, that the British cause now received a blow from which it never recovered. Burgoyne had taken part in driving the Americans from Canada in 1776 and had spent the following winter in England using his influence to secure an independent command. To his later undoing he succeeded. It was he, and not, as had been expected, General Carleton, who was appointed to lead the expedition of 1777 from Canada to the Hudson. Burgoyne was given instructions so rigid as to be an insult to his intelligence. He was to do one thing and only one thing, to press forward to the Hudson and meet Howe. At the same time Lord George Germain, the minister responsible, failed to instruct Howe to advance up the Hudson to meet Burgoyne. Burgoyne had a genuine belief in the wisdom of this strategy but he had no power to vary it, to meet changing circumstances, and this was one chief factor in his failure.

Behold Burgoyne then, on the 17th of June, embarking on Lake Champlain the army which, ever since his arrival in Canada on the 6th of May, he had been preparing for this advance. He had rather more than seven thousand men, of whom nearly one-half were Germans under the competent General Riedesel. In the force of Burgoyne we find the ominous presence of some hundreds of Indian allies. They had been attached to one side or the other in every war fought in those regions during the previous one hundred and fifty years. In the war which ended in 1763 Montcalm had used them and so had his opponent Amherst. The regiments from the New England and other colonies had fought in alliance with the painted and befeathered savages and had made no protest. Now either times had changed, or there was something in a civil war which made the use of savages seem hideous. One thing is certain. Amherst had held his savages in stern restraint and could say proudly that they had not committed a single outrage. Burgoyne was not so happy.

In nearly every war the professional soldier shows distrust, if not contempt, for civilian levies. Burgoyne had been in America before the day of Bunker Hill and knew a great deal about the country. He thought the "insurgents" good enough fighters when protected by trees and stones and swampy ground. But he thought, too, that they had no real knowledge of the science of war and could not fight a pitched battle. He himself had not shown the prevision required by sound military knowledge. If the British were going to abandon the advantage of sea power and fight where they could not fall back on their fleet, they needed to pay special attention to land transport. This Burgoyne had not done. It was only a little more than a week before he reached Lake Champlain that he asked Carleton to provide the four hundred horses and five hundred carts which he still needed and which were not easily secured in a sparsely settled country. Burgoyne lingered for three days at Crown Point, half way down the lake. Then, on the 2d of July, he laid siege to Fort Ticonderoga.

Once past this fort, guarding the route to Lake George, he could easily reach the Hudson.

In command at Fort Ticonderoga was General St. Clair, with about thirty-five hundred men. He had long notice of the siege, for the expedition of Burgoyne had been the open talk of Montreal and the surrounding country during many months. He had built Fort Independence, on the east shore of Lake Champlain, and with a great expenditure of labor had sunk twenty-two piers across the lake and stretched in front of them a boom to protect the two forts. But he had neglected to defend Sugar Hill in front of Fort Ticonderoga, and commanding the American works. It took only three or four days for the British to drag cannon to the top, erect a battery and prepare to open fire. On the 5th of July, St. Clair had to face a bitter necessity. He abandoned the untenable forts and retired southward to Fort Edward by way of the difficult Green Mountains. The British took one hundred and twenty-eight guns.

These successes led the British to think that within a few days they would be in Albany. We have an amusing picture of the effect on George III of the fall of Fort Ticonderoga. The place had been much discussed. It had been the first British fort to fall to the Americans when the Revolution began, and Carleton's failure to take it in the autumn of 1776 had been the cause of acute heart-burning in London. Now, when the news of its fall reached England, George III burst into the Queen's room with the glad cry, "I have beat them, I have beat the Americans." Washington's depression was not as great as the King's elation; he had a better sense of values; but he had intended that the fort should hold Burgoyne, and its fall was a disastrous blow. The Americans showed skill and good soldierly quality in the retreat from Ticonderoga, and Burgoyne in following and harassing them was led into hard fighting in the woods. The easier route by way of Lake George was open but Burgoyne hoped to destroy his enemy by direct pursuit through the forest. It took him twenty days to hew his way twenty miles, to the upper waters of the Hudson near Fort Edward. When there on the 30th of July he had communications open from the Hudson to the St. Lawrence.

Fortune seemed to smile on Burgoyne. He had taken many guns and he had proved the fighting quality of his men. But his cheerful elation had, in truth, no sound basis. Never during the two

and a half months of bitter struggle which followed
was he able to advance more than twenty-five
miles from Fort Edward. The moment he needed
transport by land he found himself almost helpless.
Sometimes his men were without food and equipment because he had not the horses and carts to
bring supplies from the head of water at Fort Anne
or Fort George, a score of miles away. Sometimes
he had no food to transport. He was dependent
on his communications for every form of supplies.
Even hay had to be brought from Canada, since,
in the forest country, there was little food for his
horses. The perennial problem for the British in
all operations was this one of food. The inland
regions were too sparsely populated to make it
possible for more than a few soldiers to live on
local supplies. The wheat for the bread of the
British soldier, his beef and his pork, even the oats
for his horse, came, for the most part, from England, at vast expense for transport, which made
fortunes for contractors. It is said that the cost
of a pound of salted meat delivered to Burgoyne
on the Hudson was thirty shillings. Burgoyne
had been told that the inhabitants needed only
protection to make them openly loyal and had
counted on them for supplies. He found instead

the great mass of the people hostile and he doubted the sincerity even of those who professed their loyalty.

After Burgoyne had been a month at Fort Edward he was face to face with starvation. If he advanced he lengthened his line to flank attack. As it was he had difficulty in holding it against New Englanders, the most resolute of all his foes, eager to assert by hard fighting, if need be, their right to hold the invaded territory which was claimed also by New York. Burgoyne's instructions forbade him to turn aside and strike them a heavy blow. He must go on to meet Howe who was not there to be met. A being who could see the movements of men as we watch a game of chess, might think that madness had seized the British leaders; Burgoyne on the upper Hudson plunging forward resolutely to meet Howe; Howe at sea sailing away, as it might well seem, to get as far from Burgoyne as he could; Clinton in command at New York without instructions, puzzled what to do and not hearing from his leader, Howe, for six weeks at a time; and across the sea a complacent minister, Germain, who believed that he knew what to do in a scene three thousand miles away, and had drawn up exact instructions as to the way of doing it, and who was now eagerly awaiting news of the final triumph.

Burgoyne did his best. Early in August he had to make a venturesome stroke to get sorely needed food. Some twenty-five miles east of the Hudson at Bennington, in difficult country, New England militia had gathered food and munitions, and horses for transport. The pressure of need clouded Burgoyne's judgment. To make a dash for Bennington meant a long and dangerous march. He was assured, however, that a surprise was possible and that in any case the country was full of friends only awaiting a little encouragement to come out openly on his side. They were Germans who lay on Burgoyne's left and Burgoyne sent Colonel Baum, an efficient officer, with five or six hundred men to attack the New Englanders and bring in the supplies. It was a stupid blunder to send Germans among a people specially incensed against the use of these mercenaries. There was no surprise. Many professing loyalists, seemingly eager to take the oath of allegiance, met and delayed Baum. When near Bennington he found in front of him a force barring the way and had to make a carefully guarded camp for the night. Then five hundred men, some of them the cheerful takers of the oath of allegiance, slipped round to his rear and in the morning he was attacked from front and rear.

A hot fight followed which resulted in the complete defeat of the British. Baum was mortally wounded. Some of his men escaped into the woods; the rest were killed or captured. Nor was this all. Burgoyne, scenting danger, had ordered five hundred more Germans to reinforce Baum. They, too, were attacked and overwhelmed. In all Burgoyne lost some eight hundred men and four guns. The American loss was seventy. It shows the spirit of the time that, for the sport of the soldiers, British prisoners were tied together in pairs and driven by negroes at the tail of horses. An American soldier described long after, with regret for his own cruelty, how he had taken a British prisoner who had had his left eye shot out and mounted him on a horse also without the left eye, in derision at the captive's misfortune. The British complained that quarter was refused in the fight. For days tired stragglers, after long wandering in the woods, drifted into Burgoyne's camp. This was now near Saratoga, a name destined to be ominous in the history of the British army.

Further misfortune now crowded upon Burgoyne. The general of that day had two favorite

forms of attack. One was to hold the enemy's
front and throw out a column to march round the
flank and attack his rear, the method of Howe at
the Brandywine; the other method was to advance
on the enemy by lines converging at a common
center. This form of attack had proved most
successful eighteen years earlier when the British
had finally secured Canada by bringing together,
at Montreal, three armies, one from the east, one
from the west, and one from the south. Now there
was a similar plan of bringing together three British forces at or near Albany, on the Hudson. Of
Clinton, at New York, and Burgoyne we know.
The third force was under General St. Leger. With
some seventeen hundred men, fully half of whom
were Indians, he had gone up the St. Lawrence from
Montreal and was advancing from Oswego on Lake
Ontario to attack Fort Stanwix at the end of
the road from the Great Lakes to the Mohawk
River. After taking that stronghold he intended
to go down the river valley to meet Burgoyne
near Albany.

On the 3d of August St. Leger was before Fort
Stanwix garrisoned by some seven hundred Americans. With him were two men deemed potent in
that scene. One of these was Sir John Johnson

who had recently inherited the vast estate in the neighborhood of his father, the great Indian Superintendent, Sir William Johnson, and was now in command of a regiment recruited from Loyalists, many of them fierce and embittered because of the seizure of their property. The other leader was a famous chief of the Mohawks, Thayendanegea, or, to give him his English name, Joseph Brant, half savage still, but also half civilized and half educated, because he had had a careful schooling and for a brief day had been courted by London fashion. He exerted a formidable influence with his own people. The Indians were not, however, all on one side. Half of the six tribes of the Iroquois were either neutral or in sympathy with the Americans. Among the savages, as among the civilized, the war was a family quarrel, in which brother fought brother. Most of the Indians on the American side preserved, indeed, an outward neutrality. There was no hostile population for them to plunder and the Indian usually had no stomach for any other kind of warfare. The allies of the British, on the other hand, had plenty of openings to their taste and they brought on the British cause an enduring discredit.

When St. Leger was before Fort Stanwix he

heard that a force of eight hundred men, led by a
German settler named Herkimer, was coming up
against him. When it was at Oriskany, about six
miles away, St. Leger laid a trap. He sent Brant
with some hundreds of Indians and a few soldiers
to be concealed in a marshy ravine which Herkimer must cross. When the American force was
hemmed in by trees and marsh on the narrow
causeway of logs running across the ravine the
Indians attacked with wild yells and murderous
fire. Then followed a bloody hand to hand fight.
Tradition has been busy with its horrors. Men
struggled in slime and blood and shouted curses
and defiance. Improbable stories are told of pairs
of skeletons found afterwards in the bog each with
a bony hand which had driven a knife to the heart
of the other. In the end the British, met by resolution so fierce, drew back. Meanwhile a sortie from
the American fort on their rear had a menacing
success. Sir John Johnson's camp was taken and
sacked. The two sides were at last glad to separate, after the most bloody struggle in the whole
war. St. Leger's Indians had had more than
enough. About a hundred had been killed and the
rest were in a state of mutiny. Soon it was known
that Benedict Arnold, with a considerable force,

was pushing up the Mohawk Valley to relieve the American fort. Arnold knew how to deal with savages. He took care that his friendly Indians should come into contact with those of Brant and tell lurid tales of utter disaster to Burgoyne and of a great avenging army on the march to attack St. Leger. The result was that St. Leger's Indians broke out in riot and maddened themselves with stolen rum. Disorder affected even the soldiers. The only thing for St. Leger to do was to get away. He abandoned his guns and stores and, harassed now by his former Indian allies, made his way to Oswego and in the end reached Montreal with a remnant of his force.

News of these things came to Burgoyne just after the disaster at Bennington. Since Fort Stanwix was in a country counted upon as Loyalist at heart it was especially discouraging again to find that in the main the population was against the British. During the war almost without exception Loyalist opinion proved weak against the fierce determination of the American side. It was partly a matter of organization. The vigilance committees in each State made life well-nigh intolerable to suspected Tories. Above all, however, the British had to bear the odium which attaches always to the invader. We do not know what an American army would have done if, with Iroquois savages as allies, it had made war in an English county. We know what loathing a parallel situation aroused against the British army in America. The Indians, it should be noted, were not soldiers under British discipline but allies; the chiefs regarded themselves as equals who must be consulted and not as enlisted to take orders from a British general.

In war, as in politics, nice balancing of merit or defect in an enemy would destroy the main purpose which is to defeat him. Each side exaggerates any weak point in the other in order to stimulate the fighting passions. Judgment is distorted. The Baroness Riedesel, the wife of one of Burgoyne's generals, who was in Boston in 1777, says that the people were all dressed alike in a peasant costume with a leather strap round the waist, that they were of very low and insignificant stature, and that only one in ten of them could read or write. She pictures New Englanders as tarring and feathering cultivated English ladies. When educated people believed every evil of the enemy the ignorant had no restraint to their credulity. New England had long regarded the native savages as a pest. In 1776 New Hampshire offered seventy pounds for

each scalp of a hostile male Indian and thirty-seven
pounds and ten shillings for each scalp of a woman
or of a child under twelve years of age. Now it
was reported that the British were offering bounties
for American scalps. Benjamin Franklin satirized
British ignorance when he described whales leaping
Niagara Falls and he did not expect to be taken
seriously when, at a later date, he pictured George
III as gloating over the scalps of his subjects in
America. The Seneca Indians alone, wrote Franklin, sent to the King many bales of scalps. Some
bales were captured by the Americans and they
found the scalps of 43 soldiers, 297 farmers, some of
them burned alive, and 67 old people, 88 women, 193
boys, 211 girls, 29 infants, and others unclassified.
Exact figures bring conviction. Franklin was not
wanting in exactness nor did he fail, albeit it was
unwittingly, to intensify burning resentment of
which we have echoes still. Burgoyne had to bear
the odium of the outrages by Indians. It is amusing to us, though it was hardly so to this kindly
man, to find these words put into his mouth by a
colonial poet:

> I will let loose the dogs of Hell,
> Ten thousand Indians who shall yell,
> And foam, and tear, and grin, and roar

And drench their moccasins in gore: . . .
I swear, by St. George and St. Paul,
I will exterminate you all.

Such seed, falling on soil prepared by the hate
of war, brought forth its deadly fruit. The Americans believed that there was no brutality from
which British officers would shrink. Burgoyne had
told his Indian allies that they must not kill except
in actual fighting and that there must be no slaughter of non-combatants and no scalping of any but
the dead. The warning delivered him into the
hands of his enemies for it showed that he half
expected outrage. Members of the British House
of Commons were no whit behind the Americans
in attacking him. Burke amused the House by his
satire on Burgoyne's words: "My gentle lions, my
humane bears, my tender-hearted hyenas, go forth!
But I exhort you, as you are Christians and members of civilized society, to take care not to hurt
any man, woman, or child." Burke's great speech
lasted for three and a half hours and Sir George
Savile called it "the greatest triumph of eloquence
within memory." British officers disliked their
dirty, greasy, noisy allies and Burgoyne found his
use of savages, with the futile order to be merciful,
a potent factor in his defeat.

A horrifying incident had occurred while he was fighting his way to the Hudson. As the Americans were preparing to leave Fort Edward some marauding Indians saw a chance of plunder and outrage. They burst into a house and carried off two ladies, both of them British in sympathy — Mrs. McNeil, a cousin of one of Burgoyne's chief officers, General Fraser, and Miss Jeannie McCrae, whose betrothed, a Mr. Jones, and whose brother were serving with Burgoyne. In a short time Mrs. McNeil was handed over unhurt to Burgoyne's advancing army. Miss McCrae was never again seen alive by her friends. Her body was found and a Wyandot chief, known as the Panther, showed her scalp as a trophy. Burgoyne would have been a poor creature had he not shown anger at such a crime, even if committed against the enemy. This crime, however, was committed against his own friends. He pressed the charge against the chief and was prepared to hang him and only relaxed when it was urged that the execution would cause all his Indians to leave him and to commit further outrages. The incident was appealing in its tragedy and stirred the deep anger of the population of the surrounding country among whose descendants to this day the tradition of the abandoned brutality of the British keeps alive the old hatred.

At Fort Edward Burgoyne now found that he could hardly move. He was encumbered by an enormous baggage train. His own effects filled, it is said, thirty wagons and this we can believe when we find that champagne was served at his table up almost to the day of final disaster. The population was thoroughly aroused against him. His own instinct was to remain near the water route to Canada and make sure of his communications. On the other hand, honor called him to go forward and not fail Howe, supposed to be advancing to meet him. For a long time he waited and hesitated. Meanwhile he was having increasing difficulty in feeding his army and through sickness and desertion his numbers were declining. By the 13th of September he had taken a decisive step. He made a bridge of boats and moved his whole force across the river to Saratoga, now Schuylerville. This crossing of the river would result inevitably in cutting off his communications with Lake George and Ticonderoga. After such a step he could not go back and he was moving forward into a dark unknown. The American camp was at Stillwater, twelve miles farther down the river. Burgoyne sent messenger after messenger to get past the American lines and bring back news of Howe. Not one of these unfortunate spies returned. Most of them were caught and ignominiously hanged. One thing, however, Burgoyne could do. He could hazard a fight and on this he decided as the autumn was closing in.

Burgoyne had no time to lose, once his force was on the west bank of the Hudson. General Lincoln cut off his communications with Canada and was soon laying siege to Ticonderoga. The American army facing Burgoyne was now commanded by General Gates. This Englishman, the godson of Horace Walpole, had gained by successful intrigue powerful support in Congress. That body was always paying too much heed to local claims and jealousies and on the 2d of August it removed Schuyler of New York because he was disliked by the soldiers from New England and gave the command to Gates. Washington was far away maneuvering to meet Howe and he was never able to watch closely the campaign in the north. Gates, indeed, considered himself independent of Washington and reported not to the Commander-in-Chief but direct to Congress. On the 19th of September Burgoyne attacked Gates in a strong

entrenched position on Bemis Heights, at Stillwater.
There was a long and bitter fight, but by evening Burgoyne had not carried the main position
and had lost more than five hundred men whom
he could ill spare from his scanty numbers.

Burgoyne's condition was now growing desperate.   American forces barred retreat to Canada.
He must go back and meet both frontal and flank
attacks, or go forward, or surrender.   To go forward now had most promise, for at last Howe had
instructed Clinton, left in command at New York,
to move, and Clinton was making rapid progress
up the Hudson.   On the 7th of October Burgoyne
attacked again at Stillwater.   This time he was
decisively defeated, a result due to the amazing
energy in attack of Benedict Arnold, who had been
stripped of his command by an intrigue.   Gates
would not even speak to him and his lingering in
the American camp was unwelcome.   Yet as a
volunteer Arnold charged the British line madly
and broke it.   Burgoyne's best general, Fraser,
was killed in the fight.   Burgoyne retired to Saratoga and there at last faced the prospects of getting
back to Fort Edward and to Canada.   It may be
that he could have cut his way through, but this
is doubtful.   Without risk of destruction he could

not move in any direction. His enemies now outnumbered him nearly four to one. His camp was
swept by the American guns and his men were
under arms night and day. American sharp-
shooters stationed themselves at daybreak in trees
about the British camp and any one who appeared
in the open risked his life. If a cap was held up
in view instantly two or three balls would pass
through it. His horses were killed by rifle shots.
Burgoyne had little food for his men and none for
his horses. His Indians had long since gone off in
dudgeon. Many of his Canadian French slipped
off homeward and so did the Loyalists. The German troops were naturally dispirited. A British
officer tells of the deadly homesickness of these·
poor men. They would gather in groups of two
dozen or so and mourn that they would never again
see their native land. They died, a score at a time,
of no other disease than sickness for their homes.
They could have no pride in trying to save a lost
cause. Burgoyne was surrounded and, on the 17th
of October, he was obliged to surrender.

Gates proposed to Burgoyne hard terms — surrender with no honors of war. The British were to
lay down their arms in their encampments and to
march out without weapons of any kind. Burgoyne

declared that, rather than accept such terms, he would fight still and take no quarter. A shadow was falling on the path of Gates. The term of service of some of his men had expired. The New Englanders were determined to stay and see the end of Burgoyne but a good many of the New York troops went off. Sickness, too, was increasing. Above all General Clinton was advancing up the Hudson. British ships could come up freely as far as Albany and in a few days Clinton might make a formidable advance. Gates, a timid man, was in a hurry. He therefore agreed that the British should march from their camp with the honors of war, that the troops should be taken to New England, and from there to England. They must not serve again in North America during the war but there was nothing in the terms to prevent their serving in Europe and relieving British regiments for service in America. Gates had the courtesy to keep his army where it could not see the laying down of arms by Burgoyne's force. About five thousand men, of whom sixteen hundred were Germans and only three thousand five hundred fit for duty, surrendered to sixteen thousand Americans. Burgoyne gave offense to German officers by saying in his report that he might have held out longer had all his troops been British. This is probably true but the British met with only a just Nemesis for using soldiers who had no call of duty to serve.

The army set out on its long march of two hundred miles to Boston. The late autumn weather was cold, the army was badly clothed and fed, and the discomfort of the weary route was increased by the bitter antagonism of the inhabitants. They respected the regular British soldier but at the Germans they shouted insults and the Loyalists they despised as traitors. The camp at the journey's end was on the ground at Cambridge where two years earlier Washington had trained his first army. Every day Burgoyne expected to embark. There was delay and, at last, he knew the reason. Congress repudiated the terms granted by Gates. A tangled dispute followed. Washington probably had no sympathy with the quibbling of Congress. But he had no desire to see this army return to Europe and release there an army to serve in America. Burgoyne's force was never sent to England. For nearly a year it lay at Boston. Then it was marched to Virginia. The men suffered great hardships and the numbers fell by desertion and escape. When peace came in 1783 there was no army to take back to England; Burgoyne's soldiers had been merged into the American people. It may well be, indeed, that descendants of his beaten men have played an important part in building up the United States. The irony of history is unconquerable.

CHAPTER VII

WASHINGTON AND HIS COMRADES AT VALLEY FORGE

WASHINGTON had met defeat in every considerable battle at which he was personally present. His first appearance in military history, in the Ohio campaign against the French, twenty-two years before the Revolution, was marked by a defeat, the surrender of Fort Necessity. Again in the next year, when he fought to relieve the disaster to Braddock's army, defeat was his portion. Defeat had pursued him in the battles of the Revolution — before New York, at the Brandywine, at Germantown. The campaign against Canada, which he himself planned, had failed. He had lost New York and Philadelphia. But, like William III of England, who in his long struggle with France hardly won a battle and yet forced Louis XIV to accept his terms of peace, Washington, by suddenness in reprisal, by skill in resource when his plans

148

seemed to have been shattered, grew on the hard
rock of defeat the flower of victory.

There was never a time when Washington was
not trusted by men of real military insight or by
the masses of the people. But a general who does
not win victories in the field is open to attack. By
the winter of 1777 when Washington, with his
army reduced and needy, was at Valley Forge
keeping watch on Howe in Philadelphia, John
Adams and others were talking of the sin of idola-
try in the worship of Washington, of its flavor of
the accursed spirit of monarchy, and of the punishment which "the God of Heaven and Earth" must
inflict for such perversity. Adams was all against
a Fabian policy and wanted to settle issues forever
by a short and strenuous war. The idol, it was being whispered, proved after all to have feet of clay.
One general, and only one, had to his credit a really
great victory — Gates, to whom Burgoyne had surrendered at Saratoga, and there was a movement
to replace Washington by this laureled victor.

General Conway, an Irish soldier of fortune, was
one of the most troublesome in this plot. He had
served in the campaign about Philadelphia but
had been blocked in his extravagant demands for
promotion; so he turned for redress to Gates, the

star in the north. A malignant campaign followed
in detraction of Washington. He had, it was said,
worn out his men by useless marches; with an army
three times as numerous as that of Howe, he had
gained no victory; there was high fighting quality
in the American army if properly led, but Washington despised the militia; a Gates or a Lee or a
Conway would save the cause as Washington could
not; and so on. "Heaven has determined to save
your country or a weak general and bad counsellors
would have ruined it"; so wrote Conway to Gates
and Gates allowed the letter to be seen. The words
were reported to Washington, who at once, in high
dudgeon, called Conway to account. An explosion
followed. Gates both denied that he had received
a letter with the passage in question, and, at the
same time, charged that there had been tampering
with his private correspondence. He could not
have it both ways. Conway was merely impudent
in reply to Washington, but Gates laid the whole
matter before Congress. Washington wrote to
Gates, in reply to his denials, ironical references
to "rich treasures of knowledge and experience"
"guarded with penurious reserve" by Conway
from his leaders but revealed to Gates. There was
no irony in Washington's reference to malignant

detraction and mean intrigue. At the same time he said to Gates: "My temper leads me to peace and harmony with all men," and he deplored the internal strife which injured the great cause. Conway soon left America. Gates lived to command another American army and to end his career by a crowning disaster.

Washington had now been for more than two years in the chief command and knew his problems. It was a British tradition that standing armies were a menace to liberty, and the tradition had gained strength in crossing the sea. Washington would have wished a national army recruited by Congress alone and bound to serve for the duration of the war. There was much talk at the time of a "new model army" similar in type to the wonderful creation of Oliver Cromwell. The Thirteen Colonies became, however, thirteen nations. Each reserved the right to raise its own levies in its own way. To induce men to enlist Congress was twice handicapped. First, it had no power of taxation and could only ask the States to provide what it needed. The second handicap was even greater. When Congress offered bounties to those who enlisted in the Continental army, some of the States offered higher bounties for their own levies of militia, and one authority was bidding against the other. This encouraged short-term enlistments. If a man could re-enlist and again secure a bounty, he would gain more than if he enlisted at once for the duration of the war.

An army is an intricate mechanism needing the same variety of agencies that is required for the well-being of a community. The chief aim is, of course, to defeat the enemy, and to do this an army must be prepared to move rapidly. Means of transport, so necessary in peace, are even more urgently needed in war. Thus Washington always needed military engineers to construct roads and bridges. Before the Revolution the greater part of such services had been provided in America by the regular British army, now the enemy. British officers declared that the American army was without engineers who knew the science of war, and certainly the forts on which they spent their skill in the North, those on the lower Hudson, and at Ticonderoga, at the head of Lake George, fell easily before the assailant. Good maps were needed, and in this Washington was badly served, though the defect was often corrected by his intimate knowledge of the country. Another service ill-equipped was what we should now call the Red Cross.

Epidemics, and especially smallpox, wrought havoc in the army. Then, as now, shattered nerves were sometimes the result of the strain of military life. "The wind of a ball," what we should now call shell-shock, sometimes killed men whose bodies appeared to be uninjured. To our more advanced knowledge the medical science of the time seems crude. The physicians of New England, today perhaps the most expert body of medical men in the world, were even then highly skillful. But the surgeons and nurses were too few. This was true of both sides in the conflict. Prisoners in hospitals often suffered terribly and each side brought charges of ill-treatment against the other. The prison-ships in the harbor of New York, where American prisoners were confined, became a scandal, and much bitter invective against British brutality is found in the literature of the period. The British leaders, no less than Washington himself, were humane men, and ignorance and inadequate equipment will explain most of the hardships, though an occasional officer on either side was undoubtedly callous in respect to the sufferings of the enemy.

Food and clothing, the first vital necessities of an army, were often deplorably scarce. In a land of farmers there was food enough. Its lack in the army was chiefly due to bad transport. Clothing was another matter. One of the things insisted upon in a well-trained army is a decent regard for appearance, and in the eyes of the French and the British officers the American army usually seemed rather unkempt. The formalities of dress, the uniformity of pipe-clay and powdered hair, of polished steel and brass, can of course be overdone. The British army had too much of it, but to Washington's force the danger was of having too little. It was not easy to induce farmers and frontiersmen who at home began the day without the use of water, razor, or brush, to appear on parade clean, with hair powdered, faces shaved, and clothes neat. In the long summer days the men were told to shave before going to bed that they might prepare the more quickly for parade in the morning, and to fill their canteens over night if an early march was imminent. Some of the regiments had uniforms which gave them a sufficiently smart appearance. The cocked hat, the loose hunting shirt with its fringed border, the breeches of brown leather or duck, the brown gaiters or leggings, the powdered hair, were familiar marks of the soldier of the Revolution.

During a great part of the war, however, in spite of supplies brought from both France and the West Indies, Washington found it difficult to secure for his men even decent clothing of any kind, whether of military cut or not.   More than a year after he took command, in the fighting about New York, a great part of his army had no more semblance of uniform than hunting shirts on a common pattern. In the following December, he wrote of many men as either shivering in garments fit only for summer wear or as entirely naked.   There was a time in the later campaign in the South when hundreds of American soldiers marched stark naked, except for breech cloths.   One of the most pathetic hardships of the soldier's life was due to the lack of boots. More than one of Washington's armies could be tracked by the bloody footprints of his barefooted men.   Near the end of the war Benedict Arnold, who knew whereof he spoke, described the American army as "illy clad, badly fed, and worse paid," pay being then two or three years overdue.   On the other hand, there is evidence that life in the army was not without its compensations.   Enforced dwelling in the open air saved men from diseases such as consumption and the movement from camp to camp gave a broader outlook to the farmer's sons. The army could usually make a brave parade. On ceremonial occasions the long hair of the men would be tied back and made white with powder, even though their uniforms were little more than rags.

The men carried weapons some of which, in, at any rate, the early days of the war, were made by hand at the village smithy. A man might take to the war a weapon forged by himself. The American soldier had this advantage over the British soldier, that he used, if not generally, at least in some cases, not the smooth-bore musket but the grooved rifle by which the ball was made to rotate in its flight. The fire from this rifle was extremely accurate. At first weapons were few and ammunition was scanty, but in time there were importations from France and also supplies from American gun factories. The standard length of the barrel was three and a half feet, a portentous size compared with that of the modern weapon. The loading was from the muzzle, a process so slow that one of the favorite tactics of the time was to await the fire of the enemy and then charge quickly and bayonet him before he could reload. The old method of firing off the musket by means of slow matches kept alight during action was now obsolete;

the latest device was the flintlock. But there was always a measure of doubt whether the weapon would go off. Partly on this account Benjamin Franklin, the wisest man of his time, declared for the use of the pike of an earlier age rather than the bayonet and for bows and arrows instead of fire-arms. A soldier, he said, could shoot four arrows to one bullet. An arrow wound was more disabling than a bullet wound; and arrows did not becloud the vision with smoke. The bullet remained, how-ever, the chief means of destruction, and the fire of Washington's soldiers usually excelled that of the British. These, in their turn, were superior in the use of the bayonet.

Powder and lead were hard to get. The inven-tive spirit of America was busy with plans to pro-cure saltpeter and other ingredients for making powder, but it remained scarce. Since there was no standard firearm, each soldier required bullets specially suited to his weapon. The men melted lead and cast it in their own bullet-molds. It is an instance of the minor ironies of war that the great equestrian statue of George III, which had been erected in New York in days more peaceful, was melted into bullets for killing that monarch's soldiers. Another necessity was paper for cartridges and wads. The cartridge of that day was a paper envelope containing the charge of ball and powder. This served also as a wad, after being emptied of its contents, and was pushed home with a ramrod. A store of German Bibles in Pennsylvania fell into the hands of the soldiers at a moment when paper was a crying need, and the pages of these Bibles were used for wads.

The artillery of the time seems feeble compared with the monster weapons of death which we know in our own age. Yet it was an important factor in the war. It is probable that before the war not a single cannon had been made in the colonies. From the outset Washington was hampered for lack of artillery. Neutrals, especially the Dutch in the West Indies, sold guns to the Americans, and France was a chief source of supply during long periods when the British lost the command of the sea. There was always difficulty about equipping cavalry, especially in the North. The Virginian was at home on horseback, and in the farther South bands of cavalry did service during the later years of the war, but many of the fighting riders of today might tomorrow be guiding their horses peacefully behind the plough.

The pay of the soldiers remained to Washington

a baffling problem. When the war ended their pay was still heavily in arrears. The States were timid about imposing taxation and few if any paid promptly the levies made upon them. Congress bridged the chasm in finance by issuing paper money which so declined in value that, as Washington said grimly, it required a wagon-load of money to pay for a wagon-load of supplies. The soldier received his pay in this money at its face value, and there is little wonder that the "continental dollar" is still in the United States a symbol of worthlessness. At times the lack of pay caused mutiny which would have been dangerous but for Washington's firm and tactful management in the time of crisis. There was in him both the kindly feeling of the humane man and the rigor of the army leader. He sent men to death without flinching, but he was at one with his men in their sufferings, and no problem gave him greater anxiety than that of pay, affecting, as it did, the health and spirits of men who, while unpaid, had no means of softening the daily tale of hardship.

Desertion was always hard to combat. With the homesickness which led sometimes to desertion Washington must have had a secret sympathy, for his letters show that he always longed for that

pleasant home in Virginia which he did not allow
himself to revisit until nearly the end of the war.
The land of a farmer on service often remained
untilled, and there are pathetic cases of families
in bitter need because the breadwinner was in the
army. In frontier settlements his absence sometimes meant the massacre of his family by the
savages. There is little wonder that desertion was
common, so common that after a reverse the men
went away by hundreds. As they usually carried
with them their rifles and other equipment, desertion involved a double loss. On one occasion some
soldiers undertook for themselves the punishment
of deserters. Men of the First Pennsylvania Regiment who had recaptured three deserters, beheaded
one of them and returned to their camp with the
head carried on a pole. More than once it happened that condemned men were paraded before
the troops for execution with the graves dug and
the coffins lying ready. The death sentence would
be read, and then, as the firing party took aim,
a reprieve would be announced. The reprieve
in such circumstances was omitted often enough
to make the condemned endure the real agony
of death.

Religion offered its consolations in the army and

Washington gave much thought to the service of
the chaplains. He told his army that fine as it was
to be a patriot it was finer still to be a Christian.
It is an odd fact that, though he attended the Anglican Communion service before and after the war,
he did not partake of the Communion during the
war. What was in his mind we do not know. He
was disposed, as he said himself, to let men find
"that road to Heaven which to them shall seem the
most direct," and he was without Puritan fervor,
but he had deep religious feeling. During the
troubled days at Valley Forge a neighbor came
upon him alone in the bush on his knees praying
aloud, and stole away unobserved. He would not
allow in the army a favorite Puritan custom of
burning the Pope in effigy, and the prohibition
was not easily enforced among men, thousands of
whom bore scriptural names from ancestors who
thought the Pope anti-Christ.

Washington's winter quarters at Valley Forge
were only twenty miles from Philadelphia, among
hills easily defended. It is matter for wonder that
Howe, with an army well equipped, did not make
some attempt to destroy the army of Washington which passed the winter so near and in acute

distress. The Pennsylvania Loyalists, with dark days soon to come, were bitter at Howe's inactivity, full of tragic meaning for themselves. He said that he could achieve nothing permanent by attack. It may be so; but it is a sound principle in warfare to destroy the enemy when this is possible. There was a time when in Washington's whole force not more than two thousand men were in a condition to fight. Congress was responsible for the needs of the army but was now, in sordid inefficiency, cooped up in the little town of York, eighty miles west of Valley Forge, to which it had fled. There was as yet no real federal union. The seat of authority was in the State Governments, and we need not wonder that, with the passing of the first burst of devotion which united the colonies in a common cause, Congress declined rapidly in public esteem. "What a lot of damned scoundrels we had in that second Congress" said, at a later date, Gouverneur Morris of Philadelphia to John Jay of New York, and Jay answered gravely, "Yes, we had." The body, so despised in the retrospect, had no real executive government, no organized departments. Already before Independence was proclaimed there had been talk of a permanent union, but the members of Congress had shown no

sense of urgency, and it was not until November
15, 1777, when the British were in Philadelphia and
Congress was in exile at York, that Articles of Confederation were adopted. By the following mid-
summer many of the States had ratified these
articles, but Maryland, the last to assent, did not
accept the new union until 1781, so that Congress
continued to act for the States without constitutional sanction during the greater part of the war.

The ineptitude of Congress is explained when we
recall that it was a revolutionary body which indeed controlled foreign affairs and the issues of
war and peace, coined money, and put forth paper
money but had no general powers. Each State
had but one vote, and thus a small and sparsely
settled State counted for as much as populous Massachusetts or Virginia. The Congress must deal
with each State only as a unit; it could not coerce a
State; and it had no authority to tax or to coerce
individuals. The utmost it could do was to appeal
to good feeling, and when a State felt that it had a
grievance such an appeal was likely to meet with a
flaming retort.

Washington maintained towards Congress an attitude of deference and courtesy which it did not
always deserve. The ablest men in the individual

States held aloof from Congress.   They felt that.
they had more dignity and power if they sat in
their own legislatures. The assembly which in
the first days had as members men of the type of
Washington and Franklin sank into a gathering of
second-rate men who were divided into fierce factions. They debated interminably and did little.
Each member usually felt that he must champion
the interests of his own State against the hostility
of others. It was not easy to create a sense of national life. The union was only a league of friendship. States which for a century or more had
barely acknowledged their dependence upon Great
Britain, were chary about coming under the control of a new centralizing authority at Philadelphia.
The new States were sovereign and some of them
went so far as to send envoys of their own to negotiate with foreign powers in Europe. When it was
urged that Congress should have the power to
raise taxes in the States, there were patriots who
asked sternly what the war was about if it was not
to vindicate the principle that the people of a State
alone should have power of taxation over themselves. Of New England all the other States were
jealous and they particularly disliked that proud
and censorious city which already was accused of

believing that God had made Boston for Himself and all the rest of the world for Boston. The religion of New England did not suit the Anglicans of Virginia or the Roman Catholics of Maryland, and there was resentful suspicion of Puritan intolerance. John Adams said quite openly that there were no religious teachers in Philadelphia to compare with those of Boston and naturally other colonies drew away from the severe and rather acrid righteousness of which he was a type.

Inefficiency meanwhile brought terrible suffering at Valley Forge, and the horrors of that winter remain still vivid in the memory of the American people. The army marched to Valley Forge on December 17, 1777, and in midwinter everything from houses to entrenchments had still to be created. At once there was busy activity in cutting down trees for the log huts. They were built nearly square, sixteen feet by fourteen, in rows, with the door opening on improvised streets. Since boards were scarce, and it was difficult to make roofs rainproof, Washington tried to stimulate ingenuity by offering a reward of one hundred dollars for an improved method of roofing. The fireplaces of wood were protected with thick clay.

Firewood was abundant, but, with little food for oxen and horses, men had to turn themselves into draught animals to bring in supplies.

Sometimes the army was for a week without meat. Many horses died for lack of forage or of proper care, a waste which especially disturbed Washington, a lover of horses. When quantities of clothing were ready for use, they were not delivered at Valley Forge owing to lack of transport. Washington expressed his contempt for officers who resigned their commissions in face of these distresses. No one, he said, ever heard him say a word about resignation. There were many desertions but, on the whole, he marveled at the patience of his men and that they did not mutiny. With a certain grim humor they chanted phrases about "no pay, no clothes, no provisions, no rum," and sang an ode glorifying war and Washington. Hundreds of them marched barefoot, their blood staining the snow or the frozen ground while, at the same time, stores of shoes and clothing were lying unused somewhere on the roads to the camp.

Sickness raged in the army. Few men at Valley Forge, wrote Washington, had more than a sheet, many only part of a sheet, and some nothing at all. Hospital stores were lacking. For want of straw and blankets the sick lay perishing on the frozen ground. When Washington had been at Valley Forge for less than a week, he had to report nearly three thousand men unfit for duty because of their nakedness in the bitter winter. Then, as always, what we now call the "profiteer" was holding up supplies for higher prices. To the British at Philadelphia, because they paid in gold, things were furnished which were denied to Washington at Valley Forge, and he announced that he would hang any one who took provisions to Philadelphia. To keep his men alive Washington had sometimes to take food by force from the inhabitants and then there was an outcry that this was robbery. With many sick, his horses so disabled that he could not move his artillery, and his defenses very slight, he could have made only a weak fight had Howe attacked him. Yet the legislature of Pennsylvania told him that, instead of lying quiet in winter quarters, he ought to be carrying on an active campaign. In most wars irresponsible men sitting by comfortable firesides are sure they knew best how the thing should be done.

The bleak hillside at Valley Forge was something more than a prison. Washington's staff was known as his family and his relations with them were cordial and even affectionate. The young officers faced their hardships cheerily and gave meager dinners to which no one might go if he was so well off as to have trousers without holes. They talked and sang and jested about their privations. By this time many of the bad officers, of whom Washington complained earlier, had been weeded out and he was served by a body of devoted men. There was much good comradeship. Partnership in suffering tends to draw men together. In the company which gathered about Washington, two men, mere youths at the time, have a world-wide fame. The young Alexander Hamilton, barely twenty-one years of age, and widely known already for his political writings, had the rank of lieutenant colonel gained for his services in the fighting about New York. He was now Washington's confidential secretary, a position in which he soon grew restless. His ambition was to be one of the great military leaders of the Revolution. Before the end of the war he had gone back to fighting and he distinguished himself in the last battle of the war at Yorktown. The other youthful figure was the Marquis de La Fayette. It is not without significance that a noble square bears his name in the capital named after Washington. The two men loved each other.

The young French aristocrat, with both a great
name and great possessions, was fired in 1776, when
only nineteen, with zeal for the American cause.
"With the welfare of America," he wrote to his
wife, "is closely linked the welfare of mankind."
Idealists in France believed that America was
leading in the remaking of the world. When it
was known that La Fayette intended to go to fight
in America, the King of France forbade it, since
France had as yet no quarrel with England. The
youth, however, chartered a ship, landed in South
Carolina, hurried to Philadelphia, and was a major
general in the American army when he was twenty
years of age.

La Fayette rendered no serious military service
to the American cause. He arrived in time to fight
in the battle of the Brandywine. Washington
praised him for his bravery and military ardor and
wrote to Congress that he was sensible, discreet,
and able to speak English freely. It was with
an eye to the influence in France of the name of
the young noble that Congress advanced him so
rapidly. La Fayette was sincere and generous in
spirit. He had, however, little military capacity.
Later when he might have directed the course of
the French Revolution he was found wanting in

force of character. The great Mirabeau tried to work with him for the good of France, but was repelled by La Fayette's jealous vanity, a vanity so greedy of praise that Jefferson called it a "canine appetite for popularity and fame." La Fayette once said that he had never had a thought with which he could reproach himself, and he boasted that he has mastered three kings — the King of England in the American Revolution, the King of France, and King Mob of Paris during the upheaval in France. He was useful as a diplomatist rather than as a soldier. Later, in an hour of deep need, Washington sent La Fayette to France to ask for aid. He was influential at the French court and came back with abundant promises, which were in part fulfilled.

Washington himself and Oliver Cromwell are perhaps the only two civilian generals in history who stand in the first rank as military leaders. It is doubtful indeed whether it is not rather character than military skill which gives Washington his place. Only one other general of the Revolution attained to first rank even in secondary fame. Nathanael Greene was of Quaker stock from Rhode Island. He was a natural student and when trouble with the mother country was impending

in 1774 he spent the leisure which he could spare
from his forges in the study of military history and
in organizing the local militia. Because of his zeal
for military service he was expelled from the Society of Friends. In 1775 when war broke out
he was promptly on hand with a contingent from
Rhode Island. In little more than a year and after
a very slender military experience he was in command of the army on Long Island. On the Hudson
defeat not victory was his lot. He had, however,
as much stern resolve as Washington. He shared
Washington's success in the attack on Trenton,
and his defeats at the Brandywine and at Germantown. Now he was at Valley Forge, and when, on
March 2, 1778, he became quartermaster general,
the outlook for food and supplies steadily improved. Later, in the South, he rendered brilliant
service which made possible the final American
victory at Yorktown.

Henry Knox, a Boston bookseller, had, like
Greene, only slight training for military command.
It shows the dearth of officers to fight the highly
disciplined British army that Knox, at the age of
twenty-five, and fresh from commercial life, was
placed in charge of the meager artillery which
Washington had before Boston. It was Knox, who,

with heart-breaking labor, took to the American front the guns captured at Ticonderoga. Throughout the war he did excellent service with the artillery, and Washington placed a high value upon his services. He valued too those of Daniel Morgan, an old fighter in the Indian wars, who left his farm in Virginia when war broke out, and marched his company of riflemen to join the army before Boston. He served with Arnold at the siege of Quebec, and was there taken prisoner. He was exchanged and had his due revenge when he took part in the capture of Burgoyne's army. He was now at Valley Forge. Later he had a command under Greene in the South and there, as we shall see, he won the great success of the Battle of Cowpens in January, 1781.

It was the peculiar misfortune of Washington that the three men, Arnold, Lee, and Gates, who ought to have rendered him the greatest service, proved unfaithful. Benedict Arnold, next to Washington himself, was probably the most brilliant and resourceful soldier of the Revolution. Washington so trusted him that, when the dark days at Valley Forge were over, he placed him in command of the recaptured federal capital. To-day the name of Arnold would rank high in the memory of a grateful country had he not fallen into the bottomless pit of treason. The same is in some measure true of Charles Lee, who was freed by the British in an exchange of prisoners and joined Washington at Valley Forge late in the spring of 1778. Lee was so clever with his pen as to be one of the reputed authors of the Letters of Junius. He had served as a British officer in the conquest of Canada, and later as major general in the army of Poland. He had a jealous and venomous temper and could never conceal the contempt of the professional soldier for civilian generals. He, too, fell into the abyss of treason. Horatio Gates, also a regular soldier, had served under Braddock and was thus at that early period a comrade of Washington. Intriguer he was, but not a traitor. It was incompetence and perhaps cowardice which brought his final ruin.

Europe had thousands of unemployed officers some of whom had had experience in the Seven Years' War and many turned eagerly to America for employment. There were some good soldiers among these fighting adventurers. Kosciuszko, later famous as a Polish patriot, rose by his merits to the rank of brigadier general in the American army; De Kalb, son of a German peasant, though

not a baron, as he called himself, proved worthy of
the rank of a major general. There was, however, a
flood of volunteers of another type. French officers
fleeing from their creditors and sometimes under
false names and titles, made their way to America
as best they could and came to Washington with
pretentious claims. Germans and Poles there were,
too, and also exiles from that unhappy island which
remains still the most vexing problem of British
politics. Some of them wrote their own testi-
monials; some, too, were spies. On the first day,
Washington wrote, they talked only of serving
freely a noble cause, but within a week were de-
manding promotion and advance of money. Sometimes they took a high tone with members of
Congress who had not courage to snub what
Washington called impudence and vain boasting.
"I am haunted and teased to death by the impor-
tunity of some and dissatisfaction of others" wrote
Washington of these people.

One foreign officer rendered incalculable service
to the American cause. It was not only on the
British side that Germans served in the American
Revolution. The Baron von Steuben was, like
La Fayette, a man of rank in his own country, and
his personal service to the Revolution was much

greater than that of La Fayette. Steuben had served on the staff of Frederick the Great and was distinguished for his wit and his polished manners. There was in him nothing of the needy adventurer. The sale of Hessian and other troops to the British by greedy German princes was met in some circles in Germany by a keen desire to aid the cause of the young republic. Steuben, who held a lucrative post, became convinced, while on a visit to Paris, that he could render service in training the Americans. With quick sympathy and showing no reserve in his generous spirit he abandoned his country, as it proved forever, took ship for the United States, and arrived in November, 1777. Washington welcomed him at Valley Forge in the following March. He was made Inspector General and at once took in hand the organization of the army. He prepared "Regulations for the Order and Discipline of the Troops of the United States" later, in 1779, issued as a book. Under this German influence British methods were discarded. The word of command became short and sharp. The British practice of leaving recruits to be trained by sergeants, often ignorant, coarse, and brutal, was discarded, and officers themselves did this work. The last letter which Washington wrote before he resigned his command at the end of the war was to thank Steuben for his invaluable aid. Charles Lee did not believe that American recruits could be quickly trained so as to be able to face the disciplined British battalions. Steuben was to prove that Lee was wrong to Lee's own entire undoing at Monmouth when fighting began in 1778.

The British army in America furnished sharp contrasts to that of Washington. If the British jeered at the fighting quality of citizens, these retorted that the British soldier was a mere slave. There were two great stains upon the British system, the press-gang and flogging. Press-gangs might seize men abroad in the streets of a town and, unless they could prove that they were gentlemen in rank, they could be sent in the fleet to serve in the remotest corners of the earth. In both navy and army flogging outraged the dignity of manhood. The liability to this brutal and degrading punishment kept all but the dregs of the populace from enlisting in the British army. It helped to fix the deep gulf between officers and men. Forty years later Napoleon Bonaparte, despot though he might be, was struck by this separation. He himself went freely among his men, warmed himself at their fire, and talked to them familiarly about their work, and he thought that the British officer was too aloof in his demeanor. In the British army serving in America there were many officers of aristocratic birth and long training in military science. When they found that American officers were frequently drawn from a class of society which in England would never aspire to a commission, and were largely self-taught, not unnaturally they jeered at an army so constituted. Another fact excited British disdain. The Americans were technically rebels against their lawful ruler, and rebels in arms have no rights as belligerents. When the war ended more than a thousand American prisoners were still held in England on the capital charge of treason. Nothing stirred Washington's anger more deeply than the remark sometimes made by British officers that the prisoners they took were receiving undeserved mercy when they were not hanged.

There was much debate at Valley Forge as to the prospect for the future. When we look at available numbers during the war we appreciate the view of a British officer that in spite of Washington's failures and of British victories the war was serious, "an ugly job, a damned affair indeed." The

12

population of the colonies — some 2,500,000 — was about one-third that of the United Kingdom; and for the British the war was remote from the base of supply. In those days, considering the means of transport, America was as far from England as at the present day is Australia. Sometimes the voyage across the sea occupied two and even three months, and, with the relatively small ships of the time, it required a vast array of transports to carry an army of twenty or thirty thousand men. In the spring of 1776 Great Britain had found it impossible to raise at home an army of even twenty thousand men for service in America, and she was forced to rely in large part upon mercenary soldiers. This was nothing new. Her island people did not like service abroad and this unwillingness was intensified in regard to war in remote America. Moreover Whig leaders in England discouraged enlistment. They were bitterly hostile to the war which they regarded as an attack not less on their own liberties than on those of America. It would be too much to ascribe to the ignorant British common soldier cf the time any deep conviction as to the merits or demerits of the cause for which he fought. There is no evidence that, once in the army, he was less ready to attack the Americans than any other foe. Certainly the Americans did not think he was half-hearted.

The British soldier fought indeed with more resolute determination than did the hired auxiliary at his side. These German troops played a notable part in the war. The despotic princes of the lesser German states were accustomed to sell the services of their troops. Despotic Russia, too, was a likely field for such enterprise. When, however, it was proposed to the Empress Catherine II that she should furnish twenty thousand men for service in America she retorted with the sage advice that it was England's true interest to settle the quarrel in America without war. Germany was left as the recruiting field. British efforts to enlist Germans as volunteers in her own army were promptly checked by the German rulers and it was necessary literally to buy the troops from their princes. One-fourth of the able-bodied men of Hesse-Cassel were shipped to America. They received four times the rate of pay at home and their ruler received in addition some half million dollars a year. The men suffered terribly and some died of sickness for the homes to which thousands of them never returned. German generals, such as Knyphausen and Riedesel, gave the British sincere and effective service. The Hessians were, however, of doubtful benefit to the British. It angered the Americans that hired troops should be used against them, an anger not lessened by the contempt which the Hessians showed for the colonial officers as plebeians.

The two sides were much alike in their qualities and were skillful in propaganda. In Britain lurid tales were told of the colonists scalping the wounded at Lexington and using poisoned bullets at Bunker Hill. In America every prisoner in British hands was said to be treated brutally and every man slain in the fighting to have been murdered. The use of foreign troops was a fruitful theme. The report ran through the colonies that the Hessians were huge ogre-like monsters, with double rows of teeth round each jaw, who had come at the call of the British tyrant to slay women and children. In truth many of the Hessians became good Americans. In spite of the loyalty of their officers they were readily induced to desert. The wit of Benjamin Franklin was enlisted to compose telling appeals, translated into simple German, which promised grants of land to those who should abandon an unrighteous cause. The Hessian trooper who opened a packet of tobacco might find in the wrapper appeals both to his virtue and to his cupidity. It was easy for him to resist them when the British were winning victories and he was dreaming of a return to the Fatherland with a comfortable accumulation of pay, but it was different when reverses overtook British arms. Then many hundreds slipped away; and today their blood flows in the veins of thousands of prosperous American farmers.

CHAPTER VIII

WASHINGTON badly needed aid from Europe, but there every important government was monarchical and it was not easy for a young republic, the child of revolution, to secure an ally. France tingled with joy at American victories and sorrowed at American reverses, but motives were mingled and perhaps hatred of England was stronger than love for liberty in America. The young La Fayette had a pure zeal, but he would not have fought for the liberty of colonists in Mexico as he did for those in Virginia; and the difference was that service in Mexico would not hurt the enemy of France so recently triumphant. He hated England and said so quite openly. The thought of humiliating and destroying that "insolent nation" was always to him an inspiration. Vergennes, the French Foreign Minister, though he lacked genius, was a man of boundless zeal and energy. He was at work at four o'clock in the morning and he spent his long days in toil for his country. He believed that England was the tyrant of the seas, "the monster against whom we should be always prepared," a greedy, perfidious neighbor, the natural enemy of France.

From the first days of the trouble in regard to the Stamp Act Vergennes had rejoiced that England's own children were turning against her. He had French military officers in England spying on her defenses. When war broke out he showed no nice regard for the rules of neutrality and helped the colonies in every way possible. It was a French writer who led in these activities. Beaumarchais is known to the world chiefly as the creator of the character of Figaro, which has become the type of the bold, clever, witty, and intriguing rascal, but he played a real part in the American Revolution. We need not inquire too closely into his motives. There was hatred of the English, that "audacious, unbridled, shameless people," and there was, too, the zeal for liberal ideas which made Queen Marie Antoinette herself take a pretty interest in the "dear republicans" overseas who were at the same time fighting the national enemy. Beaumarchais secured from the government money with which he purchased supplies to be sent to America. He had a great warehouse in Paris, and, under the rather fantastic Spanish name of Roderigue Hortalez & Co., he sent vast quantities of munitions and clothing to America. Cannon, not from private firms but from the government arsenals, were sent across the sea. When Vergennes showed scruples about this violation of neutrality, the answer of Beaumarchais was that governments were not bound by rules of morality applicable to private persons. Vergennes learned well the lesson and, while protesting to the British ambassador in Paris that France was blameless, he permitted outrageous breaches of the laws of neutrality.

Secret help was one thing, open alliance another. Early in 1776 Silas Deane, a member from Connecticut of the Continental Congress, was named as envoy to France to secure French aid. The day was to come when Deane should believe the struggle against Britain hopeless and counsel submission, but now he showed a furious zeal. He knew hardly a word of French, but this did not keep him from making his elaborate programme well understood. Himself a trader, he promised France vast profits from the monopoly of the trade of America when independence should be secure.

He gave other promises not more easy of fulfillment. To Frenchmen zealous for the ideals of liberty and seeking military careers in America he promised freely commissions as colonels and even generals and was the chief cause of that deluge of European officers which proved to Washington so annoying. It was through Deane's activities that La Fayette became a volunteer. Through him came too the proposal to send to America the Comte de Broglie who should be greater than colonel or general — a generalissimo, a dictator. He was to brush aside Washington, to take command of the American armies, and by his prestige and skill to secure France as an ally and win victory in the field. For such services Broglie asked only despotic power while he served and for life a great pension which would, he declared, not be one-hundredth part of his real value. That Deane should have considered a scheme so fantastic reveals the measure of his capacity, and by the end of 1776 Benjamin Franklin was sent to Paris to bring his tried skill to bear upon the problem of the alliance. With Deane and Franklin as a third member of the commission was associated Arthur Lee who had vainly sought aid at the courts of Spain and Prussia.

France was, however, coy. The end of 1776 saw the colonial cause at a very low ebb, with Washington driven from New York and about to be driven from Philadelphia. Defeat is not a good argument for an alliance. France was willing to send arms to America and willing to let American privateers use freely her ports. The ship which carried Franklin to France soon busied herself as a privateer and reaped for her crew a great harvest of prize money. In a single week of June, 1777, this ship captured a score of British merchantmen, of which more than two thousand were taken by Americans during the war. France allowed the American privateers to come and go as they liked, and gave England smooth words, but no redress. There is little wonder that England threatened to hang captured American sailors as pirates.

It was the capture of Burgoyne at Saratoga which brought decision to France. That was the victory which Vergennes had demanded before he would take open action. One British army had surrendered. Another was in an untenable position in Philadelphia. It was known that the British fleet had declined. With the best of it in America, France was the more likely to win successes in Europe. The Bourbon king of France could, too, draw into the war the Bourbon king of Spain, and Spain had good ships. The defects of France and Spain on the sea were not in ships but in men. The invasion of England was not improbable and then less than a score of years might give France both avenging justice for her recent humiliation and safety for her future. Britain should lose America, she should lose India, she should pay in a hundred ways for her past triumphs, for the arrogance of Pitt, who had declared that he would so reduce France that she should never again rise. The future should belong not to Britain but to France. Thus it was that fervent patriotism argued after the defeat of Burgoyne. Frederick the Great told his ambassador at Paris to urge upon France that she had now a chance to strike England which might never again come. France need not, he said, fear his enmity, for he was as likely to help England as the devil to help a Christian. Whatever doubts Vergennes may have entertained about an open alliance with America were now swept away. The treaty of friendship with America was signed on February 6, 1778. On the 13th of March the French ambassador in London told the British Government, with studied insolence of tone, that the United

States were by their own declaration independent.
Only a few weeks earlier the British ministry had
said that there was no prospect of any foreign intervention to help the Americans and now in the
most galling manner France told George III the
one thing to which he would not listen, that a great
part of his sovereignty was gone. Each country
withdrew its ambassador and war quickly followed.

France had not tried to make a hard bargain
with the Americans. She demanded nothing for
herself and agreed not even to ask for the restora-
tion of Canada. She required only that America
should never restore the King's sovereignty in
order to secure peace. Certain sections of opinion
in America were suspicious of France. Was she not
the old enemy who had so long harassed the fron-
tiers of New England and New York? If George
III was a despot what of Louis XVI, who had
not even an elected Parliament to restrain him?
Washington himself was distrustful of France and
months after the alliance had been concluded he
uttered the warning that hatred of England must
not lead to over-confidence in France. "No nation," he said, "is to be trusted farther than it is
bound by its interests." France, he thought, must
desire to recover Canada, so recently lost. He did

not wish to see a great military power on the northern frontier of the United States. This would be to confirm the jeer of the Loyalists that the alliance was a case of the wooden horse in Troy; the old enemy would come back in the guise of a friend and would then prove to be master and bring the colonies under a servitude compared with which the British supremacy would seem indeed mild.

The intervention of France brought a cruel embarrassment to the Whig patriot in England. He could rejoice and mourn with American patriots because he believed that their cause was his own. It was as much the interest of Norfolk as of Massachusetts that the new despotism of a king, who ruled through a corrupt Parliament, should be destroyed. It was, however, another matter when France took a share in the fight. France fought less for freedom than for revenge, and the Englishman who, like Coke of Norfolk, could daily toast Washington as the greatest of men could not link that name with Louis XVI or with his minister Vergennes. The currents of the past are too swift and intricate to be measured exactly by the observer who stands on the shore of the present, but it is arguable that the Whigs might soon have brought about peace in England had it not been for the intervention of France. No serious person any longer thought that taxation could be enforced upon America or that the colonies should be anything but free in regulating their own affairs. George III himself said that he who declared the taxing of America to be worth what it cost was "more fit for Bedlam than a seat in the Senate." The one concession Britain was not yet prepared to make was Independence. But Burke and many other Whigs were ready now for this, though Chatham still believed it would be the ruin of the British Empire.

Chatham, however, was all for conciliation, and it is not hard to imagine a group of wise men chosen from both sides, men British in blood and outlook, sitting round a table and reaching an agreement to result in a real independence for America and a real unity with Great Britain. A century and a quarter later a bitter war with an alien race in South Africa was followed by a result even more astounding. The surrender of Burgoyne had made the Prime Minister, Lord North, weary of his position. He had never been in sympathy with the King's policy and since the bad news had come in December he had pondered some radical step which should end the war. On February 17, 1778, before the treaty of friendship between the United States and France had been made public, North startled the House of Commons by introducing a bill repealing the tax on tea, renouncing forever the right to tax America, and nullifying those changes in the constitution of Massachusetts which had so rankled in the minds of its people. A commission with full powers to negotiate peace would proceed at once to America and it might suspend at its discretion, and thus really repeal, any act touching America passed since 1763.

North had taken a sharp turn. The Whig clothes had been stolen by a Tory Prime Minister and if he wished to stay in office the Whigs had not the votes to turn him out. His supporters would accept almost anything in order to dish the Whigs. They swallowed now the bill, and it became law, but at the same time came, too, the war with France. It united the Tories; it divided the Whigs. All England was deeply stirred. Nearly every important town offered to raise volunteer forces at its own expense. The Government soon had fifteen thousand men recruited at private cost. Help was offered so freely that the Whig, John Wilkes, actually introduced into Parliament a bill to prohibit gifts of money to the Crown since this voluntary taxation gave the Crown money without the consent of Parliament. The British patriot, gentle as he might be towards America, fumed against France. This was no longer only a domestic struggle between parties, but a war with an age-long foreign enemy. The populace resented what they called the insolence and the treachery of France and the French ambassador was pelted at Canterbury as he drove to the seacoast on his recall. In a large sense the French alliance was not an unmixed blessing for America, since it confused the counsels of her best friends in England.

In spite of this it is probably true that from this time the mass of the English people were against further attempts to coerce America. A change of ministry was urgently demanded. There was one leader to whom the nation looked in this grave crisis. The genius of William Pitt, Earl of Chatham, had won the last war against France and he had promoted the repeal of the Stamp Act. In America his name was held in reverence so high that New York and Charleston had erected statues in his honor. When the defeat of Burgoyne so shook the ministry that North was anxious to retire, Chatham, but for two obstacles, could probably have formed a ministry. One obstacle was

his age; as the event proved, he was near his end.
It was, however, not this which kept him from
office, but the resolve of George III. The King
simply said that he would not have Chatham.
In office Chatham would certainly rule and the
King intended himself to rule. If Chatham would
come in a subordinate position, well; but Chatham
should not lead. The King declared that as long
as even ten men stood by him he would hold out
and he would lose his crown rather than call to
office that clamorous Opposition which had attacked his American policy. "I will never consent," he said firmly, "to removing the members
of the present Cabinet from my service." He
asked North: "Are you resolved at the hour of
danger to desert me?" North remained in office.
Chatham soon died and, during four years still,
George III was master of England. Throughout
the long history of that nation there is no crisis in
which one man took a heavier and more disastrous
responsibility.

News came to Valley Forge of the alliance with
France and there were great rejoicings. We are
told that, to celebrate the occasion, Washington
dined in public. We are not given the bill of fare

in that scene of famine; but by the springtime tension in regard to supplies had been relieved and we may hope that Valley Forge really feasted in honor of the great event. The same news brought gloom to the British in Philadelphia, for it had the stern meaning that the effort and loss involved in the capture of that city were in vain. Washington held most of the surrounding country so that supplies must come chiefly by sea. With a French fleet and a French army on the way to America, the British realized that they must concentrate their defenses. Thus the cheers at Valley Forge were really the sign that the British must go.

Sir William Howe, having taken Philadelphia, was determined not to be the one who should give it up. Feeling was bitter in England over the ghastly failure of Burgoyne, and he had gone home on parole to defend himself from his seat in the House of Commons. There Howe had a seat and he, too, had need to be on hand. Lord George Germain had censured him for his course and, to shield himself, was clearly resolved to make scapegoats of others. So, on May 18, 1778, at Philadelphia there was a farewell to Howe, which took the form of a Mischianza, something approaching the medieval tournament. Knights broke lances in honor of fair ladies, there were arches and flowers and fancy costumes, and high-flown Latin and French, all in praise of the departing Howe. Obviously the garrison of Philadelphia had much time on its hands and could count upon, at least, some cheers from a friendly population. It is remembered still, with moralizings on the turns in human fortune, that Major André and Miss Margaret Shippen were the leaders in that gay scene, the one, in the days to come, to be hanged by Washington as a spy, because entrapped in the treason of Benedict Arnold, who became the husband of the other.

On May 24, 1778, Sir Henry Clinton took over from Howe the command of the British army in America and confronted a difficult problem. If d'Estaing, the French admiral, should sail straight for the Delaware he might destroy the fleet of little more than half his strength which lay there, and might quickly starve Philadelphia into surrender. The British must unite their forces to meet the peril from France, and New York, as an island, was the best point for a defense, chiefly naval. A move to New York was therefore urgent. It was by sea that the British had come to Philadelphia, but it was not easy to go away by sea. There was not room in the transports for the army and its encumbrances. Moreover, to embark the whole force, a march of forty miles to New Castle, on the lower Delaware, would be necessary and the retreating army was sure to be harassed on its way by Washington. It would besides hardly be safe to take the army by sea for the French fleet might be strong enough to capture the flotilla.

There was nothing for it but, at whatever risk, to abandon Philadelphia and march the army across New Jersey. It would be possible to take by sea the stores and the three thousand Loyalists from Philadelphia, some of whom would probably be hanged if they should be taken. Lord Howe, the naval commander, did his part in a masterly manner. On the 18th of June the British army marched out of Philadelphia and before the day was over it was across the Delaware on the New Jersey side. That same day Washington's army, free from its long exile at Valley Forge, occupied the capital. Clinton set out on his long march by land and Howe worked his laden ships down the difficult river to its mouth and, after delay by winds, put to sea on the 28th of June. By a stroke of good fortune he sailed the two hundred miles to New York in two days and missed the great fleet of d'Estaing, carrying an army of four thousand

men. On the 8th of July d'Estaing anchored at
the mouth of the Delaware. Had not his passage
been unusually delayed and Howe's unusually
quick, as Washington noted, the British fleet and
the transports in the Delaware would probably
have been taken and Clinton and his army would
have shared the fate of Burgoyne.

As it was, though Howe's fleet was clear away,
Clinton's army had a bad time in the march across
New Jersey. Its baggage train was no less than
twelve miles long and, winding along roads leading
sometimes through forests, was peculiarly vulnerable to flank attack. In this type of warfare Washington excelled. He had fought over this country
and he knew it well. The tragedy of Valley Forge
was past. His army was now well trained and well
supplied. He had about the same number of men
as the British — perhaps sixteen thousand — and
he was not encumbered by a long baggage train.
Thus it happened that Washington was across
the Delaware almost as soon as the British. He
marched parallel with them on a line some five
miles to the north and was able to forge towards
the head of their column. He could attack their
flank almost when he liked. Clinton marched with
great difficulty. He found bridges down. Not

only was Washington behind him and on his flank but General Gates was in front marching from the north to attack him when he should try to cross the Raritan River. The long British column turned southeastward toward Sandy Hook, so as to lessen the menace from Gates. Between the half of the army in the van and the other half in the rear was the baggage train.

The crisis came on Sunday the 28th of June, a day of sweltering heat. By this time General Charles Lee, Washington's second in command, was in a good position to attack the British rear guard from the north, while Washington, marching three miles behind Lee, was to come up in the hope of overwhelming it from the rear. Clinton's position was difficult but he was saved by Lee's ineptitude. He had positive instructions to attack with his five thousand men and hold the British engaged until Washington should come up in overwhelming force. The young La Fayette was with Lee. He knew what Washington had ordered, but Lee said to him: "You don't know the British soldiers; we cannot stand against them." Lee's conduct looks like deliberate treachery. Instead of attacking the British he allowed them to attack him. La Fayette managed to send a message to

Washington in the rear; Washington dashed to the front and, as he came up, met soldiers flying from before the British. He rode straight to Lee, called him in flaming anger a "damned poltroon," and himself at once took command. There was a sharp fight near Monmouth Court House. The British were driven back and only the coming of night ended the struggle. Washington was preparing to renew it in the morning, but Clinton had marched away in the darkness. He reached the coast on the 30th of June, having lost on the way fifty-nine men from sunstroke, over three hundred in battle, and a great many more by desertion. The deserters were chiefly Germans, enticed by skillful offers of land. Washington called for a reckoning from Lee. He was placed under arrest, tried by court-martial, found guilty, and suspended from rank for twelve months. Ultimately he was dismissed from the American army, less it appears for his conduct at Monmouth than for his impudent demeanor toward Congress afterwards.

These events on land were quickly followed by stirring events on the sea. The delays of the British Admiralty of this time seem almost incredible. Two hundred ships waited at Spithead for three months for convoy to the West Indies, while all the time the people of the West Indies, cut off from their usual sources of supply in America, were in distress for food. Seven weeks passed after d'Estaing had sailed for America before the Admiralty knew that he was really gone and sent Admiral Byron, with fourteen ships, to the aid of Lord Howe. When d'Estaing was already before New York Byron was still battling with storms in mid-Atlantic, storms so severe that his fleet was entirely dispersed and his flagship was alone when it reached Long Island on the 18th of August.

Meanwhile the French had a great chance. On the 11th of July their fleet, much stronger than the British, arrived from the Delaware, and anchored off Sandy Hook. Admiral Howe knew his danger. He asked for volunteers from the merchant ships and the sailors offered themselves almost to a man. If d'Estaing could beat Howe's inferior fleet, the transports at New York would be at his mercy and the British army, with no other source of supply, must surrender. Washington was near, to give help on land. The end of the war seemed not far away. But it did not come. The French admirals were often taken from an army command, and d'Estaing was not a sailor but a soldier. He feared the skill of Howe, a really great sailor, whose seven available ships were drawn up in line at Sandy Hook so that their guns bore on ships coming in across the bar. D'Estaing hovered outside. Pilots from New York told him that at high tide there were only twenty-two feet of water on the bar and this was not enough for his great ships, one of which carried ninety-one guns. On the 22d of July there was the highest of tides with, in reality, thirty feet of water on the bar, and a wind from the northeast which would have brought d'Estaing's ships easily through the channel into the harbor. The British expected the hottest naval fight in their history. At three in the afternoon d'Estaing moved but it was to sail away out of sight.

Opportunity, though once spurned, seemed yet to knock again. The one other point held by the British was Newport, Rhode Island. Here General Pigot had five thousand men and only perilous communications by sea with New York. Washington, keenly desirous to capture this army, sent General Greene to aid General Sullivan in command at Providence, and d'Estaing arrived off Newport to give aid. Greene had fifteen hundred fine soldiers, Sullivan had nine thousand New England militia, and d'Estaing four thousand

French regulars. A force of fourteen thousand five hundred men threatened five thousand British. But on the 9th of August Howe suddenly appeared near Newport with his smaller fleet. D'Estaing put to sea to fight him, and a great naval battle was imminent, when a terrific storm blew up and separated and almost shattered both fleets. D'Estaing then, in spite of American protests, insisted on taking the French ships to Boston to refit and with them the French soldiers. Sullivan publicly denounced the French admiral as having basely deserted him and his own disgusted yeomanry left in hundreds for their farms to gather in the harvest. In September, with d'Estaing safely away, Clinton sailed into Newport with five thousand men. Washington's campaign against Rhode Island had failed completely.

The summer of 1778 thus turned out badly for Washington. Help from France which had aroused such joyous hopes in America had achieved little and the allies were hurling reproaches at each other. French and American soldiers had riotous fights in Boston and a French officer was killed. The British, meanwhile, were landing at small ports on the coast, which had been the haunts of privateers, and were not only burning shipping and stores but were devastating the country with Loyalist regiments recruited in America. The French told the Americans that they were expecting too much from the alliance, and the cautious Washington expressed fear that help from outside would relax effort at home. Both were right. By the autumn the British had been reinforced and the French fleet had gone to the West Indies. Truly the mountain in labor of the French alliance seemed to have brought forth only a ridiculous mouse. None the less was it to prove, in the end, the decisive factor in the struggle.

The alliance with France altered the whole character of the war, which ceased now to be merely a war in North America. France soon gained an ally in Europe. Bourbon Spain had no thought of helping the colonies in rebellion against their king, and she viewed their ambitions to extend westward with jealous concern, since she desired for herself both sides of the Mississippi. Spain, however, had a grievance against Britain, for Britain would not yield Gibraltar, that rocky fragment of Spain commanding the entrance to the Mediterranean which Britain had wrested from her as she had wrested also Minorca and Florida.

So, in April, 1779, Spain joined France in war on Great Britain. France agreed not only to furnish an army for the invasion of England but never to make peace until Britain had handed back Gibraltar. The allies planned to seize and hold the Isle of Wight. England has often been threatened and yet has been so long free from the tramp of hostile armies that we are tempted to dismiss lightly such dangers. But in the summer of 1779 the danger was real. Of warships carrying fifty guns or more France and Spain together had one hundred and twenty-one, while Britain had seventy. The British Channel fleet for the defense of home coasts numbered forty ships of the line while France and Spain together had sixty-six. Nor had Britain resources in any other quarter upon which she could readily draw. In the West Indies she had twenty-one ships of the line while France had twenty-five. The British could not find comfort in any supposed superiority in the structure of their ships. Then and later, as Nelson admitted when he was fighting Spain, the Spanish ships were better built than the British.

Lurking in the background to haunt British thought was the growing American navy. John Paul was a Scots sailor, who had been a slave trader

and subsequently master of a West India mer-
chantman, and on going to America had assumed
the name of Jones. He was a man of boundless
ambition, vanity, and vigor, and when he commanded American privateers he became a terror
to the maritime people from whom he sprang. In
the summer of 1779 when Jones, with a squadron
of four ships, was haunting the British coasts,
every harbor was nervous. At Plymouth a boom
blocked the entrance, but other places had not
even this defense. Sir Walter Scott has described
how, on September 17, 1779, a squadron, under
John Paul Jones, came within gunshot of Leith,
the port of Edinburgh. The whole surrounding
country was alarmed, since for two days the squadron had been in sight beating up the Firth of Forth.
A sudden squall, which drove Jones back, probably
saved Edinburgh from being plundered. A few
days later Jones was burning ships in the Humber
and, on the 23d of September, he met off Flam-
borough Head and, after a desperate fight, captured two British armed ships: the *Serapis*, a 40-
gun vessel newly commissioned, and the *Countess
of Scarborough*, carrying 20 guns, both of which
were convoying a fleet. The fame of his exploit
rang through Europe. Jones was a regularly

commissioned officer in the navy of the United States,
but neutral powers, such as Holland, had not yet
recognized the republic and to them there was no
American navy. The British regarded him as a
traitor and pirate and might possibly have hanged
him had he fallen into their hands.

Terrible days indeed were these for distracted
England. In India, France, baulked twenty years
earlier, was working for her entire overthrow, and
in North Africa, Spain was using the Moors to the
same end. As time passed the storm grew more
violent. Before the year 1780 ended Holland had
joined England's enemies. Moreover, the northern
states of Europe, angry at British interference on
the sea with their trade, and especially at her
seizure of ships trying to enter blockaded ports,
took strong measures. On March 8, 1780, Russia
issued a proclamation declaring that neutral ships
must be allowed to come and go on the sea as they
liked. They might be searched by a nation at
war for arms and ammunition but for nothing else.
It would moreover be illegal to declare a blockade
of a port and punish neutrals for violating it, unless
their ships were actually caught in an attempt to
enter the port. Denmark and Sweden joined Russia
in what was known as the Armed Neutrality and

promised that they would retaliate upon any nation which did not respect the conditions laid down.

In domestic affairs Great Britain was divided. The Whigs and Tories were carrying on a warfare shameless beyond even the bitter partisan strife of later days. In Parliament the Whigs cheered at military defeats which might serve to discredit the Tory Government. The navy was torn by faction. When, in 1778, the Whig Admiral Keppel fought an indecisive naval battle off Ushant and was afterwards accused by one of his officers, Sir Hugh Palliser, of not pressing the enemy hard enough, party passion was invoked. The Whigs were for Keppel, the Tories for Palliser, and the London mob was Whig. When Keppel was acquitted there were riotous demonstrations; the house of Palliser was wrecked, and he himself barely escaped with his life. Whig naval officers declared that they had no chance of fair treatment at the hands of a Tory Admiralty, and Lord Howe, among others, now refused to serve. For a time British supremacy on the sea disappeared and it was only regained in April, 1782, when the Tory Admiral Rodney won a great victory in the West Indies against the French.

A spirit of violence was abroad in England. The

disabilities of the Roman Catholics were a gross scandal. They might not vote or hold public office. Yet when, in 1780, Parliament passed a bill removing some of their burdens dreadful riots broke out in London. A fanatic, Lord George Gordon, led a mob to Westminster and, as Dr. Johnson expressed it, "insulted" both Houses of Parliament. The cowed ministry did nothing to check the disturbance. The mob burned Newgate jail, released the prisoners from this and other prisons, and made a deliberate attempt to destroy London by fire. Order was restored under the personal direction of the King, who, with all his faults, was no coward. At the same time the Irish Parliament, under Protestant lead, was making a Declaration of Independence which, in 1782, England was obliged to admit by formal act of Parliament. For the time being, though the two monarchies had the same king, Ireland, in name at least, was free of England.

Washington's enemy thus had embarrassments enough. Yet these very years, 1779 and 1780, were the years in which he came nearest to despair. The strain of a great movement is not in the early days of enthusiasm, but in the slow years when idealism is tempered by the strife of opinion and self-interest which brings delay and disillusion. As the war went on recruiting became steadily more difficult. The alliance with France actually worked to discourage it since it was felt that the cause was safe in the hands of this powerful ally. Whatever Great Britain's difficulties about finance they were light compared with Washington's. In time the "continental dollar" was worth only two cents. Yet soldiers long had to take this money at its face value for their pay, with the result that the pay for three months would scarcely buy a pair of boots. There is little wonder that more than once Washington had to face formidable mutiny among his troops. The only ones on whom he could rely were the regulars enlisted by Congress and carefully trained. The worth of the militia, he said, "depends entirely on the prospects of the day; if favorable, they throng to you; if not, they will not move." They played a chief part in the prosperous campaign of 1777, when Burgoyne was beaten. In the next year, before Newport, they wholly failed General Sullivan and deserted shamelessly to their homes.

By 1779 the fighting had shifted to the South. Washington personally remained in the North to guard the Hudson and to watch the British in

14

New York. He sent La Fayette to France in January, 1779, there to urge not merely naval but military aid on a great scale. La Fayette came back after an absence of a little over a year and in the end France promised eight thousand men who should be under Washington's control as completely as if they were American soldiers. The older nation accepted the principle that the officers in the younger nation which she was helping should rank in their grade before her own. It was a magnanimity reciprocated nearly a century and a half later when a great American army in Europe was placed under the supreme command of a Marshal of France.

CHAPTER IX

THE WAR IN THE SOUTH

AFTER 1778 there was no more decisive fighting in the North. The British plan was to hold New York and keep there a threatening force, but to make the South henceforth the central arena of the war. Accordingly, in 1779, they evacuated Rhode Island and left the magnificent harbor of Newport to be the chief base for the French fleet and army in America. They also drew in their posts on the Hudson and left Washington free to strengthen West Point and other defenses by which he was blocking the river. Meanwhile they were striking staggering blows in the South. On December 29, 1778, a British force landed two miles below Savannah, in Georgia, lying near the mouth of the important Savannah River, and by nightfall, after some sharp fighting, took the place with its stores and shipping. Augusta, the capital of Georgia, lay about a hundred and twenty-five miles up the river. By the end of February, 1779, the British not only held Augusta but had established so strong a line of posts in the interior that Georgia seemed to be entirely under their control.

Then followed a singular chain of events. Ever since hostilities had begun, in 1775, the revolutionary party had been dominant in the South. Yet now again in 1779 the British flag floated over the capital of Georgia. Some rejoiced and some mourned. Men do not change lightly their political allegiance. Probably Boston was the most completely revolutionary of American towns. Yet even in Boston there had been a sad procession of exiles who would not turn against the King. The South had been more evenly divided. Now the Loyalists took heart and began to assert themselves.

When the British seemed secure in Georgia bands of Loyalists marched into the British camp in furious joy that now their day was come, and gave no gentle advice as to the crushing of rebellion. Many a patriot farmhouse was now destroyed and the hapless owner either killed or driven to the mountains to live as best he could by hunting. Sometimes even the children were shot down. It so happened that a company of militia captured a large band of Loyalists marching to Augusta to

support the British cause. Here was the occasion
for the republican patriots to assert their principles. To them these Loyalists were guilty of
treason. Accordingly seventy of the prisoners
were tried before a civil court and five of them
were hanged. For this hanging of prisoners the
Loyalists, of course, retaliated in kind. Both the
British and American regular officers tried to restrain these fierce passions but the spirit of the
war in the South was ruthless. To this day many
a tale of horror is repeated and, since Loyalist
opinion was finally destroyed, no one survived to
apportion blame to their enemies. It is probable
that each side matched the other in barbarity.

The British hoped to sweep rapidly through the
South, to master it up to the borders of Virginia,
and then to conquer that breeding ground of revolution. In the spring of 1779 General Prevost
marched from Georgia into South Carolina. On
the 12th of May he was before Charleston de-
manding surrender. We are astonished now to
read that, in response to Prevost's demand, a proposal was made that South Carolina should be
allowed to remain neutral and that at the end of
the war it should join the victorious side. This
certainly indicates a large body of opinion which

was not irreconcilable with Great Britain and seems to justify the hope of the British that the beginnings of military success might rally the mass of the people to their side. For the moment, however, Charleston did not surrender. The resistance was so stiff that Prevost had to raise the siege and go back to Savannah.

Suddenly, early in September, 1779, the French fleet under d'Estaing appeared before Savannah. It had come from the West Indies, partly to avoid the dreaded hurricane season of the autumn in those waters. The British, practically without any naval defense, were confronted at once by twenty-two French ships of the line, eleven frigates, and many transports carrying an army. The great flotilla easily got rid of the few British ships lying at Savannah. An American army, under General Lincoln, marched to join d'Estaing. The French landed some three thousand men, and the combined army numbered about six thousand. A siege began which, it seemed, could end in only one way. Prevost, however, with three thousand seven hundred men, nearly half of them sick, was defiant, and on the 9th of October the combined French and American armies made a great assault. They met with disaster. D'Estaing was severely wounded.

With losses of some nine hundred killed and
wounded in the bitter fighting the assailants drew
off and soon raised the siege. The British losses
were only fifty-four. In the previous year French
and Americans fighting together had utterly failed.
Now they had failed again and there was bitter
recrimination between the defeated allies. D'Estaing sailed away and soon lost some of his ships
in a violent storm. Ill-fortune pursued him to the
end. He served no more in the war and in the
Reign of Terror in Paris, in 1794, he perished on
the scaffold.

At Charleston the American General Lincoln
was in command with about six thousand men.
The place, named after King Charles II, had been
a center of British influence before the war. That
critical traveler, Lord Adam Gordon, thought its
people clever in business, courteous, and hospit-
able. Most of them, he says, made a visit to England at some time during life and it was the fashion
to send there the children to be educated. Obviously Charleston was fitted to be a British rallying center in the South; yet it had remained in
American hands since the opening of the war. In
1776 Sir Henry Clinton, the British Commander,
had woefully failed in his assault on Charleston.

Now in December, 1779, he sailed from New York
to make a renewed effort. With him were three of
his best officers — Cornwallis, Simcoe, and Tarleton, the last two skillful leaders of irregulars, recruited in America and used chiefly for raids.
The wintry voyage was rough; one of the vessels
laden with cannon foundered and sank, and all the
horses died. But Clinton reached Charleston and
was able to surround it on the landward side with
an army at least ten thousand strong. Tarleton's
irregulars rode through the country. It is on
record that he marched sixty-four miles in twenty-
three hours and a hundred and five miles in fifty-
four hours. Such mobility was irresistible. On
the 12th of April, after a ride of thirty miles, Tarleton surprised, in the night, three regiments of
American cavalry regulars at a place called Biggin's Bridge, routed them completely and, according to his own account, with the loss of three men
wounded, carried off a hundred prisoners, four
hundred horses, and also stores and ammunition.
There is no doubt that Tarleton's dragoons behaved with great brutality and it would perhaps
have taught a needed lesson if, as was indeed
threatened by a British officer, Major Ferguson, a
few of them had been shot on the spot for these

outrages.   Tarleton's dashing attacks isolated
Charleston and there was nothing for Lincoln to
do but to surrender.   This he did on the 12th of
May.   Burgoyne seemed to have been avenged.
The most important city in the South had fallen.
"We look on America as at our feet," wrote Horace
Walpole.   The British advanced boldly into the
interior.   On the 29th of May Tarleton attacked
an American force under Colonel Buford, killed
over a hundred men, carried off two hundred prisoners, and had only twenty-one casualties.   It is
such scenes that reveal the true character of the
war in the South.   Above all it was a war of hard
riding, often in the night, of sudden attack, and
terrible bloodshed.

   After the fall of Charleston only a few American
irregulars were to be found in South Carolina.   It
and Georgia seemed safe in British control.   With
British successes came the problem of governing
the South.   On the royalist theory, the recovered
land had been in a state of rebellion and was now
restored to its true allegiance.   Every one who had
taken up arms against the King was guilty of
treason with death as the penalty.   Clinton had no
intention of applying this hard theory, but he was
returning to New York and he had to establish a

government on some legal basis. During the first years of the war, Loyalists who would not accept the new order had been punished with great severity. Their day had now come. Clinton said that "every good man" must be ready to join in arms the King's troops in order "to reëstablish peace and good government." "Wicked and desperate men" who still opposed the King should be punished with rigor and have their property confiscated. He offered pardon for past offenses, except to those who had taken part in killing Loyalists "under the mock forms of justice." No one was henceforth to be exempted from the active duty of supporting the King's authority.

Clinton's proclamation was very disturbing to the large element in South Carolina which did not desire to fight on either side. Every one must now be for or against the King, and many were in their secret hearts resolved to be against him. There followed an orgy of bloodshed which discredits human nature. The patriots fled to the mountains rather than yield and, in their turn, waylaid and murdered straggling Loyalists. Under pressure some republicans would give outward compliance to royal government, but they could not be coerced into a real loyalty. It required only a reverse to

the King's forces to make them again actively
hostile. To meet the difficult situation Congress
now made a disastrous blunder. On June 13, 1780,
General Gates, the belauded victor at Saratoga,
was given the command in the South.

Camden, on the Wateree River, lies inland from
Charleston about a hundred and twenty-five miles
as the crow flies. The British had occupied it soon
after the fall of Charleston, and it was now held by
a small force under Lord Rawdon, one of the ablest
of the British commanders. Gates had superior
numbers and could probably have taken Camden
by a rapid movement; but the man had no real
stomach for fighting. He delayed until, on the
14th of August, Cornwallis arrived at Camden with
reinforcements and with the fixed resolve to attack
Gates before Gates attacked him. On the early
morning of the 16th of August, Cornwallis with
two thousand men marching northward between
swamps on both flanks, met Gates with three
thousand marching southward, each of them in-
tending to surprise the other. A fierce struggle
followed. Gates was completely routed with a
thousand casualties, a thousand prisoners, and the
loss of nearly the whole of his guns and transport.
The fleeing army was pursued for twenty miles by

the relentless Tarleton. General Kalb, who had done much to organize the American army, was killed. The enemies of Gates jeered at his riding away with the fugitives and hardly drawing rein until after four days he was at Hillsborough, two hundred miles away. His defense was that he "proceeded with all possible despatch," which he certainly did, to the nearest point where he could reorganize his forces. His career was, however, ended. He was deprived of his command, and Washington appointed to succeed him General Nathanael Greene.

In spite of the headlong flight of Gates the disaster at Camden had only a transient effect. The war developed a number of irregular leaders on the American side who were never beaten beyond recovery, no matter what might be the reverses of the day. The two most famous are Francis Marion and Thomas Sumter. Marion, descended from a family of Huguenot exiles, was slight in frame and courteous in manner; Sumter, tall, powerful, and rough, was the vigorous frontiersman in type. Threatened men live long: Sumter died in 1832, at the age of ninety-six, the last surviving general of the Revolution. Both men had had prolonged experience in frontier fighting against the Indians

Tarleton called Marion the "old swamp fox" because he often escaped through using by-paths across the great swamps of the country. British communications were always in danger. A small British force might find itself in the midst of a host which had suddenly come together as an army, only to dissolve next day into its elements of hardy farmers, woodsmen, and mountaineers.

After the victory at Camden Cornwallis advanced into North Carolina, and sent Major Ferguson, one of his most trusted officers, with a force of about a thousand men, into the mountainous country lying westward, chiefly to secure Loyalist recruits. If attacked in force Ferguson was to retreat and rejoin his leader. The Battle of King's Mountain is hardly famous in the annals of the world, and yet, in some ways, it was a decisive event. Suddenly Ferguson found himself beset by hostile bands, coming from the north, the south, the east, and the west. When, in obedience to his orders, he tried to retreat he found the way blocked, and his messages were intercepted, so that Cornwallis was not aware of the peril. Ferguson, harassed, outnumbered, at last took refuge on King's Mountain, a stony ridge on the western border between the two Carolinas. The north side of the mountain was a sheer impassable cliff and, since the ridge was only half a mile long, Ferguson thought that his force could hold it securely. He was, however, fighting an enemy deadly with the rifle and accustomed to fire from cover. The sides and top of King's Mountain were wooded and strewn with boulders. The motley assailants crept up to the crest while pouring a deadly fire on any of the defenders who exposed themselves. Ferguson was killed and in the end his force surrendered, on October 7, 1780, with four hundred casualties and the loss of more than seven hundred prisoners. The American casualties were eighty-eight. In reprisal for earlier acts on the other side, the victors insulted the dead body of Ferguson and hanged nine of their prisoners on the limb of a great tulip tree. Then the improvised army scattered.[1]

While the conflict for supremacy in the South was still uncertain, in the Northwest the Americans made a stroke destined to have astounding results. Virginia had long coveted lands in the valleys of the Ohio and the Mississippi. It was in this region that Washington had first seen active service, helping to wrest that land from France. The

[1] See Chapter IX, *Pioneers of the Old Southwest*, by Constance Lindsay Skinner in *The Chronicles of America*.

country was wild.   There was almost no settlement; but over a few forts on the upper Mississippi
and in the regions lying eastward to the Detroit
River there was that flicker of a red flag which
meant that the Northwest was under British rule.
George Rogers Clark, like Washington a Virginian
land surveyor, was a strong, reckless, brave frontiersman.   Early in 1778 Virginia gave him a small
sum of money, made him a lieutenant colonel, and
authorized him to raise troops for a western ad-
venture.   He had less than two hundred men when
he appeared a little later at Kaskaskia near the
Mississippi in what is now Illinois and captured
the small British garrison, with the friendly consent
of the French settlers about the fort.   He did the
same thing at Cahokia, farther up the river.   The
French scattered through the western country
naturally sided with the Americans, fighting now
in alliance with France.   The British sent out a
force from Detroit to try to check the efforts of
Clark, but in February, 1779, the indomitable
frontiersman surprised and captured this force at
Vincennes on the Wabash.   Thus did Clark's two
hundred famished and ragged men take possession
of the Northwest, and, when peace was made, this
vast domain, an empire in extent, fell to the United

States. Clark's exploit is one of the pregnant romances of history.[1]

Perhaps the most sorrowful phase of the Revolution was the internal conflict waged between its friends and its enemies in America, where neighbor fought against neighbor. During this pitiless struggle the strength of the Loyalists tended steadily to decline; and they came at last to be regarded everywhere by triumphant revolution as a vile people who should bear the penalties of outcasts. In this attitude towards them Boston had given a lead which the rest of the country eagerly followed. To coerce Loyalists local committees sprang up everywhere. It must be said that the Loyalists gave abundant provocation. They sneered at rebel officers of humble origin as convicts and shoe-blacks. There should be some fine hanging, they promised, on the return of the King's men to Boston. Early in the Revolution British colonial governors, like Lord Dunmore of Virginia, adopted the policy of reducing the rebels by harrying their coasts. Sailors would land at night from ships and commit their ravages in the light of burning houses. Soldiers would dart out beyond the British lines,

[1] See Chapters III and IV in *The Old Northwest* by Frederic Austin Ogg in *The Chronicles of America*.

burn a village, carry off some Whig farmers, and
escape before opposing forces could rally. Governor Tryon of New York was specially active in
these enterprises and to this day a special odium
attaches to his name.

For these ravages, and often with justice, the
Loyalists were held responsible. The result was a
bitterness which fired even the calm spirit of Benjamin Franklin and led him when the day came
for peace to declare that the plundering and mur-
dering adherents of King George were the ones who
should pay for damage and not the States which
had confiscated Loyalist property. Lists of Loyalist names were sometimes posted and then the persons concerned were likely to be the victims of any
one disposed to mischief. Sometimes a suspected
Loyalist would find an effigy hung on a tree before
his own door with a hint that next time the figure might be himself. A musket ball might come
whizzing through his window. Many a Loyalist was stripped, plunged in a barrel of tar, and
then rolled in feathers, taken sometimes from his
own bed.

Punishment for loyalism was not, however, left
merely to chance. Even before the Declaration of
Independence, Congress, sitting itself in a city

15

where loyalism was strong, urged the States to act sternly in repressing Loyalist opinion. They did not obey every urging of Congress as eagerly as they responded to this one. In practically every State Test Acts were passed and no one was safe who did not carry a certificate that he was free of any suspicion of loyalty to King George. Magistrates were paid a fee for these certificates and thus had a golden reason for insisting that Loyalists should possess them. To secure a certificate the holder must forswear allegiance to the King and promise support to the State at war with him. An unguarded word even about the value in gold of the continental dollar might lead to the adding of the speaker's name to the list of the proscribed. Legislatures passed bills denouncing Loyalists. The names in Massachusetts read like a list of the leading families of New England. The "Black List" of Pennsylvania contained four hundred and ninety names of Loyalists charged with treason, and Philadelphia had the grim experience of seeing two Loyalists led to the scaffold with ropes around their necks and hanged. Most of the persecuted Loyalists lost all their property and remained exiles from their former homes. The self-appointed committees took in hand the task of disciplining those who did not fly, and the rabble often pushed matters to brutal extremes. When we remember that Washington himself regarded Tories as the vilest of mankind and unfit to live, we can imagine the spirit of mobs, which had sometimes the further incentive of greed for Loyalist property. Loyalists had the experience of what we now call boycotting when they could not buy or sell in the shops and were forced to see their own shops plundered. Mills would not grind their corn. Their cattle were maimed and poisoned. They could not secure payment of debts due to them or, if payment was made, they received it in the debased continental currency at its face value. They might not sue in a court of law, nor sell their property, nor make a will. It was a felony for them to keep arms. No Loyalist might hold office, or practice law or medicine, or keep a school.

Some Loyalists were deported to the wilderness in the back country. Many took refuge within the British lines, especially at New York. Many Loyalists created homes elsewhere. Some went to England only to find melancholy disillusion of hope that a grateful motherland would understand and reward their sacrifices. Large numbers found their way to Nova Scotia and to Canada, north of the

Great Lakes, and there played a part in laying the foundation of the Dominion of today. The city of Toronto with a population of half a million is rooted in the Loyalist traditions of its Tory founders. Simcoe, the first Governor of Upper Canada, who made Toronto his capital, was one of the most enterprising of the officers who served with Cornwallis in the South and surrendered with him at Yorktown.

The State of New York acquired from the forfeited lands of Loyalists a sum approaching four million dollars, a great amount in those days. Other States profited in a similar way. Every Loyalist whose property was seized had a direct and personal grievance. He could join the British army and fight against his oppressors, and this he did: New York furnished about fifteen thousand men to fight on the British side. Plundered himself, he could plunder his enemies, and this too he did both by land and sea. In the autumn of 1778 ships manned chiefly by Loyalist refugees were terrorizing the coast from Massachusetts to New Jersey. They plundered Martha's Vineyard, burned some lesser towns, such as New Bedford, and showed no quarter to small parties of American troops whom they managed to intercept.

What happened on the coast happened also in the interior. At Wyoming in the northeastern part of Pennsylvania, in July, 1778, during a raid of Loyalists, aided by Indians, there was a brutal massacre, the horrors of which long served to inspire hate for the British. A little later in the same year similar events took place at Cherry Valley, in central New York. Burning houses, the dead bodies not only of men but of women and children scalped by the savage allies of the Loyalists, desolation and ruin in scenes once peaceful and happy — such horrors American patriotism learned to associate with the Loyalists. These in their turn remembered the slow martyrdom of their lives as social outcasts, the threats and plunder which in the end forced them to fly, the hardships, starvation, and death to their loved ones which were wont to follow. The conflict is perhaps the most tragic and irreconcilable in the whole story of the Revolution.

CHAPTER X

DURING 1778 and 1779 French effort had failed.
Now France resolved to do something decisive. She
never sent across the sea the eight thousand men
promised to La Fayette but by the spring of 1780
about this number were gathered at Brest to find
that transport was inadequate. The leader was
a French noble, the Comte de Rochambeau, an old
campaigner, now in his fifty-fifth year, who had
fought against England before in the Seven Years'
War and had then been opposed by Clinton, Cornwallis, and Lord George Germain. He was a sound
and prudent soldier who shares with La Fayette
the chief glory of the French service in America.
Rochambeau had fought at the second battle of
Minden, where the father of La Fayette had fallen,
and he had for the ardent young Frenchman the
amiable regard of a father and sometimes rebuked
his impulsiveness in that spirit. He studied the

problem in America with the insight of a trained leader. Before he left France he made the pregnant comment on the outlook: "Nothing without naval supremacy." About the same time Washington was writing to La Fayette that a decisive naval supremacy was a fundamental need.

A gallant company it was which gathered at Brest. Probably no other land than France could have sent forth on a crusade for democratic liberty a band of aristocrats who had little thought of applying to their own land the principles for which they were ready to fight in America. Over some of them hung the shadow of the guillotine; others were to ride the storm of the French Revolution and to attain fame which should surpass their sanguine dreams. Rochambeau himself, though he narrowly escaped during the Reign of Terror, lived to extreme old age and died a Marshal of France. Berthier, one of his officers, became one of Napoleon's marshals and died just when Napoleon, whom he had deserted, returned from Elba. Dumas became another of Napoleon's generals. He nearly perished in the retreat from Moscow but lived, like Rochambeau, to extreme old age. One of the gayest of the company was the Duc de Lauzun, a noted libertine in France but, as far as the record goes, a man of blameless propriety in America. He died on the scaffold during the French Revolution. So, too, did his companion, the Prince de Broglie, in spite of the protest of his last words that he was faithful to the principles of the Revolution, some of which he had learned in America. Another companion was the Swedish Count Fersen, later the devoted friend of the unfortunate Queen Marie Antoinette, the driver of the carriage in which the royal family made the famous flight to Varennes in 1791, and himself destined to be trampled to death by a Swedish mob in 1810. Other old and famous names there were: Laval-Montmorency, Mirabeau, Talleyrand, Saint-Simon. It has been said that the names of the French officers in America read like a list of medieval heroes in the Chronicles of Froissart.

Only half of the expected ships were ready at Brest and only five thousand five hundred men could embark. The vessels were, of course, very crowded. Rochambeau cut down the space allowed for personal effects. He took no horse for himself and would allow none to go, but he permitted a few dogs. Forty-five ships set sail, "a truly imposing sight," said one of those on board. We have reports of their *ennui* on the long voyage of seventy days, of their amusements and their devotions, for twice daily were prayers read on deck. They sailed into Newport on the 11th of July and the inhabitants of that still primitive spot illuminated their houses as best they could. Then the army settled down at Newport and there it remained for many weary months. Reinforcements never came, partly through mismanagement in France, partly through the vigilance of the British fleet, which was on guard before Brest. The French had been for generations the deadly enemies of the English Colonies and some of the French officers noted the reserve with which they were received. The ice was, however, soon broken. They brought with them gold, and the New England merchants liked this relief from the debased continental currency. Some of the New England ladies were beautiful, and the experienced Lauzun expresses glowing admiration for a prim Quakeress whose simple dress he thought more attractive than the elaborate modes of Paris.

The French dazzled the ragged American army by their display of waving plumes and of uniforms in striking colors. They wondered at the quantities of tea drunk by their friends and so do we when we remember the political hatred for tea. They made the blunder common in Europe of thinking that there were no social distinctions in America. Washington could have told him a different story. Intercourse was at first difficult, for few of the Americans spoke French and fewer still of the French spoke English. Sometimes the talk was in Latin, pronounced by an American scholar as not too bad. A French officer writing in Latin to an American friend announces his intention to learn English: "*Inglicam linguam noscere conabor.*" He made the effort and he and his fellow officers learned a quaint English speech. When Rochambeau and Washington first met they conversed through La Fayette, as interpreter, but in time the older man did very well in the language of his American comrade in arms.

For a long time the French army effected nothing. Washington longed to attack New York and urged the effort, but the wise and experienced Rochambeau applied his principle, "nothing without naval supremacy," and insisted that in such an attack a powerful fleet should act with a powerful army, and, for the moment, the French had no powerful fleet available. The British were blockading in Narragansett Bay the French fleet which lay there. Had the French army moved away from Newport their fleet would almost certainly have become a prey to the British. For the moment there was nothing to do but to wait. The French preserved an admirable discipline. Against their army there are no records of outrage and plunder such as we have against the German allies of the British. We must remember, however, that the French were serving in the country of their friends, with every restraint of good feeling which this involved. Rochambeau told his men that there must not be the theft of a bit of wood, or of any vegetables, or of even a sheaf of straw. He threatened the vice which he called "sonorous drunkenness," and even lack of cleanliness, with sharp punishment. The result was that a month after landing he could say that not a cabbage had been stolen. Our credulity is strained when we are told that apple trees with their fruit overhung the tents of his soldiers and remained untouched. Thousands flocked to see the French camp. The bands played and Puritan maidens of all grades of society danced with the young French officers and we are told, whether we believe it or not, that there was the simple innocence of the Garden of Eden. The zeal of the French officers and the friendly disposition of the men never failed. There had been bitter quarrels in 1778 and 1779 and now the French were careful to be on their good behavior in America. Rochambeau had been instructed tc place himself under the command of Washington, to whom were given the honors of a Marshal of France. The French admiral, had, however, been given no such instructions and Washington had no authority over the fleet.

Meanwhile events were happening which might have brought a British triumph. On September 14, 1780, there arrived and anchored at Sandy Hook, New York, fourteen British ships of the line under Rodney, the doughtiest of the British admirals afloat. Washington, with his army headquarters at West Point, on guard to keep the British from advancing up the Hudson, was looking for the arrival, not of a British fleet, but of a French fleet, from the West Indies. For him these were very dark days. The recent defeat at Camden was a crushing blow. Congress was inept and had in it men, as the patient General Greene said, "without principles, honor or modesty." The coming of the British fleet was a new and overwhelming discouragement, and, on the 18th of September, Washington left West Point for a long ride to Hartford in Connecticut, half way between the two headquarters, there to take counsel with the French general. Rochambeau, it was said, had been purposely created to understand Washington, but as yet the two leaders had not met. It is the simple truth that Washington had to go to the French as a beggar. Rochambeau said later that Washington was afraid to reveal the extent of his distress. He had to ask for men and for ships, but he had also to ask for what a proud man dislikes to ask, for money from the stranger who had come to help him.

The Hudson had long been the chief object of Washington's anxiety and now it looked as if the British intended some new movement up the river, as indeed they did. Clinton had not expected Rodney's squadron, but it arrived opportunely and, when it sailed up to New York from Sandy Hook, on the 16th of September, he began at once to embark his army, taking pains at the same time to send out reports that he was going to the Chesapeake. Washington concluded that the opposite was true and that he was likely to be going northward. At West Point, where the Hudson flows through a mountainous gap, Washington had strong defenses on both shores of the river. His batteries commanded its whole width, but shore batteries were ineffective against moving ships. The embarking of Clinton's army meant that he planned operations on land. He might be going to Rhode Island or to Boston but he might also dash up the Hudson. It was an anxious leader who, with La Fayette and Alexander Hamilton, rode away from headquarters to Hartford.

The officer in command at West Point was Benedict Arnold. No general on the American side had a more brilliant record or could show more scars of battle. We have seen him leading an army through the wilderness to Quebec, and incurring hardships almost incredible. Later he is found on Lake Champlain, fighting on both land and water. When in the next year the Americans succeeded at Saratoga it was Arnold who bore the brunt of the fighting. At Quebec and again at Saratoga he was severely wounded. In the summer of 1778 he was given the command at Philadelphia, after the British evacuation. It was a troubled time. Arnold was concerned with confiscations of property for treason and with disputes about ownership. Impulsive, ambitious, and with a certain element of coarseness in his nature, he made enemies. He was involved in bitter strife with both Congress

and the State government of Pennsylvania. After
a period of tension and privation in war, one of
slackness and luxury is almost certain to follow.
Philadelphia, which had recently suffered for want
of bare necessities, now relapsed into gay indul-
gence. Arnold lived extravagantly. He played
a conspicuous part in society and, a widower of
thirty-five, was successful in paying court to Miss
Shippen, a young lady of twenty, with whom, as
Washington said, all the American officers were
in love.

Malignancy was rampant and Arnold was pursued with great bitterness. Joseph Reed, the
President of the Executive Council of Pennsylvania, not only brought charge against him of
abusing his position for his own advantage, but
also laid the charges before each State government.
In the end Arnold was tried by court-martial and
after long and inexcusable delay, on January
26, 1780, he was acquitted of everything but the
imprudence of using, in an emergency, public
wagons to remove private property, and of grant-
ing irregularly a pass to a ship to enter the port of
Philadelphia. Yet the court ordered that for these
trifles Arnold should receive a public reprimand
from the Commander-in-Chief. Washington gave

the reprimand in terms as gentle as possible, and when, in July, 1780, Arnold asked for the important command at West Point, Washington readily complied probably with relief that so important a position should be in such good hands.

The treason of Arnold now came rapidly to a head. The man was embittered. He had rendered great services and yet had been persecuted with spiteful persistence. The truth seems to be, too, that Arnold thought America ripe for reconciliation with Great Britain. He dreamed that he might be the saviour of his country. Monk had reconciled the English republic to the restored Stuart King Charles II; Arnold might reconcile the American republic to George III for the good of both. That reconciliation he believed was widely desired in America. He tried to persuade himself that to change sides in this civil strife was no more culpable then to turn from one party to another in political life. He forgot, however, that it is never honorable to betray a trust.

It is almost certain that Arnold received a large sum in money for his treachery. However this may be, there was treason in his heart when he asked for and received the command at West Point, and he intended to use his authority to surrender that vital post to the British. And now on the 18th of September Washington was riding northeastward into Connecticut, British troops were on board ships in New York and all was ready. On the 20th of September the *Vulture*, sloop of war, sailed up the Hudson from New York and anchored at Stony Point, a few miles below West Point. On board the *Vulture* was the British officer who was treating with Arnold and who now came to arrange terms with him, Major John André, Clinton's young adjutant general, a man of attractive personality. Under cover of night Arnold sent off a boat to bring André ashore to a remote thicket of fir trees, outside the American lines. There the final plans were made. The British fleet, carrying an army, was to sail up the river. A heavy chain had been placed across the river at West Point to bar the way of hostile ships. Under pretense of repairs a link was to be taken out and replaced by a rope which would break easily. The defenses of West Point were to be so arranged that they could not meet a sudden attack and Arnold was to surrender with his force of three thousand men. Such a blow following the disasters at Charleston and Camden might end the strife. Britain was prepared to yield everything but

16

separation; and America, Arnold said, could now make an honorable peace.

A chapter of accidents prevented the testing. Had André been rowed ashore by British tars they could have taken him back to the ship at his command before daylight. As it was the American boatmen, suspicious perhaps of the meaning of this talk at midnight between an American officer and a British officer, both of them in uniform, refused to row André back to the ship because their own return would be dangerous in daylight. Contrary to his instructions and wishes André accompanied Arnold to a house within the American lines to wait until he could be taken off under cover of night. Meanwhile, however, an American battery on shore, angry at the *Vulture*, lying defiantly within range, opened fire upon her and she dropped down stream some miles. This was alarming. Arnold, however, arranged with a man to row André down the river and about midday went back to West Point.

It was uncertain how far the *Vulture* had gone. The vigilance of those guarding the river was aroused and André's guide insisted that he should go to the British lines by land. He was carrying compromising papers and wearing civilian dress when seized by an American party and held under close arrest. Arnold meanwhile, ignorant of this delay, was waiting for the expected advance up the river of the British fleet. He learned of the arrest of André while at breakfast on the morning of the twenty-fifth, waiting to be joined by Washington, who had just ridden in from Hartford. Arnold received the startling news with extraordinary composure, finished the subject under discussion, and then left the table under pretext of a summons from across the river. Within a few minutes his barge was moving swiftly to the *Vulture* eighteen miles away. Thus Arnold escaped. The unhappy André was hanged as a spy on the 2d of October. He met his fate bravely. Washington, it is said, shed tears at its stern necessity under military law. Forty years later the bones of André were reburied in Westminster Abbey, a tribute of pity for a fine officer.

The treason of Arnold is not in itself important, yet Washington wrote with deep conviction that Providence had directly intervened to save the American cause. Arnold might be only one of many. Washington said, indeed, that it was a wonder there were not more. In a civil war every one of importance is likely to have ties with both sides, regrets for the friends he has lost, misgivings in respect to the course he has adopted. In April, 1779, Arnold had begun his treason by expressing discontent at the alliance with France then working so disastrously. His future lay before him; he was still under forty; he had just married into a family of position; he expected that both he and his descendants would spend their lives in America and he must have known that contempt would follow them for the conduct which he planned if it was regarded by public opinion as base. Voices in Congress, too, had denounced the alliance with France as alliance with tyranny, political and religious. Members praised the liberties of England and had declared that the Declaration of Independence must be revoked and that now it could be done with honor since the Americans had proved their metal. There was room for the fear that the morale of the Americans was giving way.

The defection of Arnold might also have military results. He had bargained to be made a general in the British army and he had intimate knowledge of the weak points in Washington's position. He advised the British that if they would do two things, offer generous terms to soldiers serving in the American army, and concentrate their effort, they could win the war. With a cynical knowledge of the weaker side of human nature, he declared that it was too expensive a business to bring men from England to serve in America. They could be secured more cheaply in America; it would be necessary only to pay them better than Washington could pay his army. As matters stood the Continental troops were to have half pay for seven years after the close of the war and grants of land ranging from one hundred acres for a private to eleven hundred acres for a general. Make better offers than this, urged Arnold; "Money will go farther than arms in America." If the British would concentrate on the Hudson where the defenses were weak they could drive a wedge between North and South. If on the other hand they preferred to concentrate in the South, leaving only a garrison in New York, they could overrun Virginia and Maryland and then the States farther south would give up a fight in which they were already beaten. Energy and enterprise, said Arnold, will quickly win the war.

In the autumn of 1780 the British cause did, indeed, seem near triumph. An election in England in October gave the ministry an increased majority and with this renewed determination.

When Holland, long a secret enemy, became an open one in December, 1780, Admiral Rodney descended on the Dutch island of St. Eustatius, in the West Indies, where the Americans were in the habit of buying great quantities of stores and on the 3d of February, 1781, captured the place with two hundred merchant ships, half a dozen men-of-war, and stores to the value of three million pounds. The capture cut off one chief source of supply to the United States. By January, 1781, a crisis in respect to money came to a head. Fierce mutinies broke out because there was no money to provide food, clothing, or pay for the army and the men were in a destitute condition. "These people are at the end of their resources," wrote Rochambeau in March. Arnold's treason, the halting voices in Congress, the disasters in the South, the British success in cutting off supplies of stores from St. Eustatius, the sordid problem of money — all these were well fitted to depress the worn leader so anxiously watching on the Hudson. It was the dark hour before the dawn.

CHAPTER XI

THE critical stroke of the war was near. In the South, after General Greene superseded Gates in the command, the tide of war began to turn. Cornwallis now had to fight a better general than Gates. Greene arrived at Charlotte, North Carolina, in December. He found an army badly equipped, wretchedly clothed, and confronted by a greatly superior force. He had, however, some excellent officers, and he did not scorn, as Gates, with the stiff military traditions of a regular soldier, had scorned, the aid of guerrilla leaders like Marion and Sumter. Serving with Greene was General Daniel Morgan, the enterprising and resourceful Virginia rifleman, who had fought vaiorously at Quebec, at Saratoga, and later in Virginia. Steuben was busy in Virginia holding the British in check and keeping open the line of communication with the North. The mobility and diversity of the

American forces puzzled Cornwallis. When he marched from Camden into North Carolina he hoped to draw Greene into a battle and to crush him as he had crushed Gates. He sent Tarleton with a smaller force to strike a deadly blow at Morgan who was threatening the British garrisons at the points in the interior farther south. There was no more capable leader than Tarleton; he had won many victories; but now came his day of defeat. On January 17, 1781, he met Morgan at the Cowpens, about thirty miles west from King's Mountain. Morgan, not quite sure of the discipline of his men, stood with his back to a broad river so that retreat was impossible. Tarleton had marched nearly all night over bad roads; but, confident in the superiority of his weary and hungry veterans, he advanced to the attack at daybreak. The result was a complete disaster. Tarleton himself barely got away with two hundred and seventy men and left behind nearly nine hundred casualties and prisoners.

Cornwallis had lost one-third of his effective army. There was nothing for him to do but to take his loss and still to press on northward in the hope that the more southerly inland posts could take care of themselves. In the early spring of 1781.

when heavy rains were making the roads difficult and the rivers almost impassable, Greene was luring Cornwallis northward and Cornwallis was chasing Greene. At Hillsborough, in the northwest corner of North Carolina, Cornwallis issued a proclamation saying that the colony was once more under the authority of the King and inviting the Loyalists, bullied and oppressed during nearly six years, to come out openly on the royal side. On the 15th of March Greene took a stand and offered battle at Guilford Court House. In the early afternoon, after a march of twelve miles without food, Cornwallis, with less than two thousand men, attacked Greene's force of about four thousand. By evening the British held the field and had captured Greene's guns. But they had lost heavily and they were two hundred miles from their base. Their friends were timid, and in fact few, and their numerous enemies were filled with passionate resolution.

Cornwallis now wrote to urge Clinton to come to his aid. Abandon New York, he said; bring the whole British force into Virginia and end the war by one smashing stroke; that would be better than sticking to salt pork in New York and sending only enough men to Virginia to steal tobacco.

Cornwallis could not remain where he was, far from the sea. Go back to Camden he would not after a victory, and thus seem to admit a defeat. So he decided to risk all and go forward. By hard marching he led his army down the Cape Fear River to Wilmington on the sea, and there he arrived on the 9th of April. Greene, however, simply would not do what Cornwallis wished — stay in the north to be beaten by a second smashing blow. He did what Cornwallis would not do; he marched back into the South and disturbed the British dream that now the country was held securely. It mattered little that, after this, the British won minor victories. Lord Rawdon, still holding Camden, defeated Greene on the 25th of April at Hobkirk's Hill. None the less did Rawdon find his position untenable and he, too, was forced to march to the sea, which he reached at a point near Charleston. Augusta, the capital of Georgia, fell to the Americans on the 5th of June and the operations of the summer went decisively in their favor. The last battle in the field of the farther South was fought on the 8th of September at Eutaw Springs, about fifty miles northwest of Charleston. The British held their position and thus could claim a victory. But it was fruitless

They had been forced steadily to withdraw. All the boasted fabric of royal government in the South had come down with a crash and the Tories who had supported it were having evil days.

While these events were happening farther south, Cornwallis himself, without waiting for word from Clinton in New York, had adopted his own policy and marched from Wilmington northward into Virginia. Benedict Arnold was now in Virginia doing what mischief he could to his former friends. In January he burned the little town of Richmond, destined in the years to come to be a great center in another civil war. Some twenty miles south from Richmond lay in a strong position Petersburg, later also to be drenched with blood shed in civil strife. Arnold was already at Petersburg when Cornwallis arrived on the 20th of May. He was now in high spirits. He did not yet realize the extent of the failure farther south. Virginia he believed to be half loyalist at heart. The negroes would, he thought, turn against their masters when they knew that the British were strong enough to defend them. Above all he had a finely disciplined army of five thousand men. Cornwallis was the more confident when he knew by whom he was opposed. In April Washington had placed La

Fayette in charge of the defense of Virginia, and not only was La Fayette young and untried in such a command but he had at first only three thousand badly-trained men to confront the formidable British general. Cornwallis said cheerily that "the boy" was certainly now his prey and began the task of catching him.

An exciting chase followed. La Fayette did some good work. It was impossible, with his inferior force, to fight Cornwallis, but he could tire him out by drawing him into long marches. When Cornwallis advanced to attack La Fayette at Richmond, La Fayette was not there but had slipped away and was able to use rivers and mountains for his defense. Cornwallis had more than one string to his bow. The legislature of Virginia was sitting at Charlottesville, lying in the interior nearly a hundred miles northwest from Richmond, and Cornwallis conceived the daring plan of raiding Charlottesville, capturing the Governor of Virginia, Thomas Jefferson, and, at one stroke, shattering the civil administration. Tarleton was the man for such an enterprise of hard riding and bold fighting and he nearly succeeded. Jefferson indeed escaped by rapid flight but Tarleton took the town, burned the public records, and captured ammunition and arms. But he really effected little. La Fayette was still unconquered. His army was growing and the British were finding that Virginia, like New England, was definitely against them.

At New York, meanwhile, Clinton was in a dilemma. He was dismayed at the news of the march of Cornwallis to Virginia. Cornwallis had been so long practically independent in the South that he assumed not only the right to shape his own policy but adopted a certain tartness in his despatches to Clinton, his superior. When now, in this tone, he urged Clinton to abandon New York and join him Clinton's answer on the 26th of June was a definite order to occupy some port in Virginia easily reached from the sea, to make it secure, and to send to New York reinforcements. The French army at Newport was beginning to move towards New York and Clinton had intercepted letters from Washington to La Fayette revealing a serious design to make an attack with the aid of the French fleet. Such was the game which fortune was playing with the British generals. Each desired the other to abandon his own plans and to come to his aid. They were agreed, however, that some strong point must be held in Virginia as a naval base, and on the 2d of August

Cornwallis established this base at Yorktown, at the mouth of the York River, a mile wide where it flows into Chesapeake Bay. His cannon could command the whole width of the river and keep in safety ships anchored above the town. Yorktown lay about half way between New York and Charleston and from here a fleet could readily carry a military force to any needed point on the sea. La Fayette with a growing army closed in on Yorktown, and Cornwallis, almost before he knew it, was besieged with no hope of rescue except by a fleet.

Then it was that from the sea, the restless and mysterious sea, came the final decision. Man seems so much the sport of circumstance that apparent trifles, remote from his consciousness, appear at times to determine his fate; it is a commonplace of romance that a pretty face or a stray bullet has altered the destiny not merely of families but of nations. And now, in the American Revolution, it was not forts on the Hudson, nor maneuvers in the South, that were to decide the issue, but the presence of a few more French warships than the British could muster at a given spot and time. Washington had urged in January that France should plan to have at least temporary naval superiority in American waters, in accordance with Rochambeau's principle, "Nothing without naval supremacy." Washington wished to concentrate against New York, but the French were of a different mind, believing that the great effort should be made in Chesapeake Bay. There the British could have no defenses like those at New York, and the French fleet, which was stationed in the West Indies, could reach more readily than New York a point in the South.

Early in May Rochambeau knew that a French fleet was coming to his aid but not yet did he know where the stroke should be made. It was clear, however, that there was nothing for the French to do at Newport, and, by the beginning of June, Rochambeau prepared to set his army in motion. The first step was to join Washington on the Hudson and at any rate alarm Clinton as to an imminent attack on New York and hold him to that spot. After nearly a year of idleness the French soldiers were delighted that now at last there was to be an active movement. The long march from Newport to New York began. In glowing June, amid the beauties of nature, now overcome by intense heat and obliged to march at two o'clock in the morning, now drenched by heavy rains, the French plodded on, and joined their American comrades along the Hudson early in July.

By the 14th of August Washington knew two things — that a great French fleet under the Comte de Grasse had sailed for the Chesapeake and that the British army had reached Yorktown. Soon the two allied armies, both lying on the east side of the Hudson, moved southward. On the 20th of August the Americans began to cross the river at King's Ferry, eight miles below Peekskill. Washington had to leave the greater part of his army before New York, and his meager force of some two thousand was soon over the river in spite of torrential rains. By the 24th of August the French, too, had crossed with some four thousand men and with their heavy equipment. The British made no move. Clinton was, however, watching these operations nervously. The united armies marched down the right bank of the Hudson so rapidly that they had to leave useful effects behind and some grumbled at the privation. Clinton thought his enemy might still attack New York from the New Jersey shore. He knew that near Staten Island the Americans were building great bakeries as if to feed an army besieging New York. Suddenly on the 29th of August the armies turned away from New York southwestward across New Jersey, and still only the two leaders knew whither they were bound.

American patriotism has liked to dwell on this last great march of Washington. To him this was familiar country; it was here that he had harassed Clinton on the march from Philadelphia to New York three long years before. The French marched on the right at the rate of about fifteen miles a day. The country was beautiful and the roads were good. Autumn had come and the air was bracing. The peaches hung ripe on the trees. The Dutch farmers who, four years earlier, had been plaintive about the pillage by the Hessians, now seemed prosperous enough and brought abundance of provisions to the army. They had just gathered their harvest. The armies passed through Princeton, with its fine college, numbering as many as fifty students; then on to Trenton, and across the Delaware to Philadelphia, which the vanguard reached on the 3d of September.

There were gala scenes in Philadelphia. Twenty thousand people witnessed a review of the French army. To one of the French officers the city seemed "immense" with its seventy-two streets all "in a straight line." The shops appeared to be

I

equal to those of Paris and there were pretty
women well dressed in the French fashion. The
Quaker city forgot its old suspicion of the French
and their Catholic religion. Luzerne, the French
Minister, gave a great banquet on the evening of
the 5th of September. Eighty guests took their
places at table and as they sat down good news
arrived. As yet few knew the destination of the
army but now Luzerne read momentous tidings
and the secret was out: twenty-eight French snips
of the line had arrived in Chesapeake Bay; an
army of three thousand men had already dis-
embarked and was in touch with the army of
La Fayette; Washington and Rochambeau were
bound for Yorktown to attack Cornwallis. Great
was the joy; in the streets the soldiers and the
people shouted and sang and humorists, mounted on chairs, delivered in advance mock funeral
orations on Cornwallis.

It was planned that the army should march the
fifty miles to Elkton, at the head of Chesapeake
Bay, and there take boat to Yorktown, two hundred miles to the south at the other end of the Bay.
But there were not ships enough. Washington had
asked the people of influence in the neighborhood
to help him to gather transports but few of them

responded. A deadly apathy in regard to the war seems to have fallen upon many parts of the country. The Bay now in control of the French fleet was quite safe for unarmed ships. Half the Americans and some of the French embarked and the rest continued on foot. There was need of haste, and the troops marched on to Baltimore and beyond at the rate of twenty miles a day, over roads often bad and across rivers sometimes unbridged. At Baltimore some further regiments were taken on board transports and most of them made the final stages of the journey by water. Some there were, however, and among them the Vicomte de Noailles, brother-in-law of La Fayette, who tramped on foot the whole seven hundred and fifty-six miles from Newport to Yorktown. Washington himself left the army at Elkton and rode on with Rochambeau, making about sixty miles a day. Mount Vernon lay on the way and here Washington paused for two or three days. It was the first time he had seen it since he set out on May 4, 1775, to attend the Continental Congress at Philadelphia, little dreaming then of himself as chief leader in a long war. Now he pressed on to join La Fayette. By the end of the month an army of sixteen thousand men, of whom about one-half were French, was besieging Cornwallis with seven thousand men in Yorktown.

Heart-stirring events had happened while the armies were marching to the South. The Comte de Grasse, with his great fleet, arrived at the entrance to the Chesapeake on the 30th of August while the British fleet under Admiral Graves still lay at New York. Grasse, now the pivot upon which everything turned, was the French admiral in the West Indies. Taking advantage of a lull in operations he had slipped away with his whole fleet, to make his stroke and be back again before his absence had caused great loss. It was a risky enterprise, but a wise leader takes risks. He intended to be back in the West Indies before the end of October.

It was not easy for the British to realize that they could be outmatched on the sea. Rodney had sent word from the West Indies that ten ships were the limit of Grasse's numbers and that even fourteen British ships would be adequate to meet him. A British fleet, numbering nineteen ships of the line, commanded by Admiral Graves, left New York on the 31st of August and five days later stood off the entrance to Chesapeake Bay. On the mainland across the Bay lay Yorktown, the one point now held by the British on that great stretch of coast. When Graves arrived he had an unpleasant surprise. The strength of the French had been well concealed. There to confront him lay twenty-four enemy ships. The situation was even worse, for the French fleet from Newport was on its way to join Grasse.

On the afternoon of the 5th of September, the day of the great rejoicing in Philadelphia, there was a spectacle of surpassing interest off Cape Henry, at the mouth of the Bay. The two great fleets joined battle, under sail, and poured their fire into each other. When night came the British had about three hundred and fifty casualties and the French about two hundred. There was no brilliant leadership on either side. One of Graves's largest ships, the *Terrible*, was so crippled that he burnt her, and several others were badly damaged. Admiral Hood, one of Graves's officers, says that if his leader had turned suddenly and anchored his ships across the mouth of the Bay, the French Admiral with his fleet outside would probably have sailed away and left the British fleet in possession. As it was the two fleets lay at sea in sight of each other for four days. On the morning of the tenth the squadron from Newport under Barras arrived and increased Grasse's ships to thirty-six. Against such odds Graves could do nothing. He lingered near the mouth of the Chesapeake for a few days still and then sailed away to New York to refit. At the most critical hour of the whole war a British fleet, crippled and spiritless, was hurrying to a protecting port and the fleurs-de-lis waved unchallenged on the American coast. The action of Graves spelled the doom of Cornwallis. The most potent fleet ever gathered in those waters cut him off from rescue by sea.

Yorktown fronted on the York River with a deep ravine and swamps at the back of the town. From the land it could on the west side be approached by a road leading over marshes and easily defended, and on the east side by solid ground about half a mile wide now protected by redoubts and entrenchments with an outer and an inner parallel. Could Cornwallis hold out? At New York, no longer in any danger, there was still a keen desire to rescue him. By the end of September he received word from Clinton that reinforcements had arrived from England and that, with a fleet of twenty-six ships of the line carrying five thousand troops, he hoped to sail on the 5th of October to the rescue of Yorktown. There was delay. Later Clinton wrote that on the basis of assurances from Admiral Graves he hoped to get away on the twelfth. A British officer in New York describes the hopes with which the populace watched these preparations. The fleet, however, did not sail until the 19th of October. A speaker in Congress at the time said that the British Admiral should certainly hang for this delay.

On the 5th of October, for some reason unexplained, Cornwallis abandoned the outer parallel and withdrew behind the inner one. This left him in Yorktown a space so narrow that nearly every part of it could be swept by enemy artillery. By the 11th of October shells were dropping incessantly from a distance of only three hundred yards, and before this powerful fire the earthworks crumbled. On the fourteenth the French and Americans carried by storm two redoubts on the second parallel. The redoubtable Tarleton was in Yorktown, and he says that day and night there was acute danger to any one showing himself and that every gun was dismounted as soon as seen. He was for evacuating the place and marching away, whither he hardly knew. Cornwallis still held Gloucester, on the opposite side of the York River, and he now planned to cross to that place with his best troops, leaving behind his sick and wounded. He would try to reach Philadelphia by the route over which Washington had just ridden. The feat was not impossible. Washington would have had a stern chase in following Cornwallis, who might have been able to live off the country. Clinton could help by attacking Philadelphia, which was almost defenseless.

As it was, a storm prevented the crossing to Gloucester. The defenses of Yorktown were weakening and in face of this new discouragement the British leader made up his mind that the end was near. Tarleton and other officers condemned Cornwallis sharply for not persisting in the effort to get away. Cornwallis was a considerate man. "I thought it would have been wanton and inhuman," he reported later, "to sacrifice the lives of this small body of gallant soldiers." He had already written to Clinton to say that there would be great risk in trying to send a fleet and army to rescue him. On the 19th of October came the climax. Cornwallis surrendered with some hundreds of sailors and about seven thousand soldiers. of whom two thousand were in hospital. The terms were similar to those which the British had granted at Charleston to General Lincoln, who was now charged with carrying out the surrender.

Such is the play of human fortune. At two o'clock in the afternoon the British marched out between two lines, the French on the one side, the Americans on the other, the French in full dress uniform, the Americans in some cases half naked and barefoot. No civilian sightseers were admitted, and there was a respectful silence in the presence of this great humiliation to a proud army. The town itself was a dreadful spectacle with, as a French observer noted, "big holes made by bombs, cannon balls, splinters, barely covered graves, arms and legs of blacks and whites scattered here and there, most of the houses riddled with shot and devoid of window-panes."

On the very day of surrender Clinton sailed from New York with a rescuing army. Nine days later forty-four British ships were counted off the entrance to Chesapeake Bay. The next day there were none. The great fleet had heard of the surrender and had turned back to New York. Washington urged Grasse to attack New York or Charleston but the French Admiral was anxious to take his fleet back to meet the British menace farther south and he sailed away with all his great array. The waters of the Chesapeake, the scene of one of the decisive events in human history,

were deserted by ships of war. Grasse had sailed,
however, to meet a stern fate. He was a fine fighting sailor. His men said of him that he was on
ordinary days six feet in height but on battle days
six feet and six inches. None the less did a few
months bring the British a quick revenge on the
sea. On April 12, 1782, Rodney met Grasse in
a terrible naval battle in the West Indies. Some
five thousand in both fleets perished. When night
came Grasse was Rodney's prisoner and Britain
had recovered her supremacy on the sea. On returning to France Grasse was tried by court-martial and, though acquitted, he remained in dis-
grace until he died in 1788, "weary," as he said,
"of the burden of life." The defeated Cornwallis
was not blamed in England. His character commanded wide respect and he lived to play a great
part in public life. He became Governor General of India, and was Viceroy of Ireland when its
restless union with England was brought about
in 1800.

Yorktown settled the issue of the war but did
not end it. For more than a year still hostilities
continued and, in parts of the South, embittered
faction led to more bloodshed. In England the

news of Yorktown caused a commotion. When
Lord George Germain received the first despatch
he drove with one or two colleagues to the Prime
Minister's house in Downing Street. A friend
asked Lord George how Lord North had taken the
news. "As he would have taken a ball in the
breast," he replied; "for he opened his arms, ex-
claiming wildly, as he paced up and down the
apartment during a few minutes, 'Oh God! it is all
over,' words which he repeated many times, under
emotions of the deepest agitation and distress."
Lord North might well be agitated for the news
meant the collapse of a system. The King was at
Kew and word was sent to him. That Sunday
evening Lord George Germain had a small dinner
party and the King's letter in reply was brought
to the table. The guests were curious to know how
the King took the news. "The King writes just
as he always does," said Lord George, "except that
I observe he has omitted to mark the hour and the
minute of his writing with his usual precision."
It needed a heavy shock to disturb the routine of
George III. The King hoped no one would think
that the bad news "makes the smallest alteration
in those principles of my conduct which have
directed me in past time." Lesser men might

change in the face of evils; George III was resolved
to be changeless and never, never, to yield to the
coercion of facts.

Yield, however, he did. The months which
followed were months of political commotion in
England. For a time the ministry held its majority
against the fierce attacks of Burke and Fox. The
House of Commons voted that the war must go on.
But the heart had gone out of British effort.
Everywhere the people were growing restless.
Even the ministry acknowledged that the war in
America must henceforth be defensive only. In
February, 1782, a motion in the House of Com-
mons for peace was lost by only one vote; and in
March, in spite of the frantic expostulations of the
King, Lord North resigned. The King insisted
that at any rate some members of the new ministry
must be named by himself and not, as is the Brit-
ish constitutional custom, by the Prime Minister.
On this, too, he had to yield; and a Whig ministry,
under the Marquis of Rockingham, took office
in March, 1782. Rockingham died on the 1st of
July, and it was Lord Shelburne, later the Marquis
of Lansdowne, under whom the war came to an end.
The King meanwhile declared that he would return to Hanover rather than yield the independence

of the colonies. Over and over again he had
said that no one should hold office in his government who would not pledge himself to keep the
Empire entire. But even his obstinacy was broken.
On December 5, 1782, he opened Parliament with
a speech in which the right of the colonies to in·
dependence was acknowledged. "Did I lower my
voice when I came to that part of my speech?"
George asked afterwards. He might well speak in
a subdued tone for he had brought the British
Empire to the lowest level in its history.

In America, meanwhile, the glow of victory had
given way to weariness and lassitude. Rochambeau with his army remained in Virginia. Washington took his forces back to the lines before New
York, sparing what men he could to help Greene
in the South. Again came a long period of watching
and waiting. Washington, knowing the obstinate
determination of the British character, urged Congress to keep up the numbers of the army so as to
be prepared for any emergency. Sir Guy Carleton
now commanded the British at New York and
Washington feared that this capable Irishman
might soothe the Americans into a false security.
He had to speak sharply, for the people seemed in-
different to further effort and Congress was slack

and impotent. The outlook for Washington's allies in the war darkened, when in April, 1782, Rodney won his crushing victory and carried De Grasse a prisoner to England. France's ally Spain had been besieging Gibraltar for three years, but in September, 1782, when the great battering-ships specially built for the purpose began a furious bombardment, which was expected to end the siege, the British defenders destroyed every ship, and after that Gibraltar was safe. These events naturally stiffened the backs of the British in negotiating peace. Spain declared that she would never make peace without the surrender of Gibraltar, and she was ready to leave the question of American independence undecided or decided against the colonies if she could only get for herself the terms which she desired. There was a period when France seemed ready to make peace on the basis of dividing the Thirteen States, leaving some of them independent while others should remain under the British King.

Congress was not willing to leave its affairs at Paris in the capable hands of Franklin alone. In 1780 it sent John Adams to Paris, and John Jay and Henry Laurens were also members of the American Commission. The austere Adams disliked and was jealous of Franklin, gay in spite of his years, seemingly indolent and easygoing, always bland and reluctant to say No to any request from his friends, but ever astute in the interests of his country. Adams told Vergennes, the French foreign minister, that the Americans owed nothing to France, that France had entered the war in her own interests, and that her alliance with America had greatly strengthened her position in Europe. France, he added, was really hostile to the colonies, since she was jealously trying to keep them from becoming rich and powerful. Adams dropped hints that America might be compelled to make a separate peace with Britain. When it was proposed that the depreciated continental paper money, largely held in France for purchases there, should be redeemed at the rate of one good dollar for every forty in paper money, Adams declared to the horrified French creditors of the United States that the proposal was fair and just. At the same time Congress was drawing on Franklin in Paris for money to meet its requirements and Franklin was expected to persuade the French treasury to furnish him with what he needed and to an amazing degree succeeded in doing so. The self interest which Washington believed to be the dominant

motive in politics was, it is clear, actively at
work. In the end the American Commissioners
negotiated directly with Great Britain, without
asking for the consent of their French allies. On
November 30, 1782, articles of peace between
Great Britain and the United States were signed.
They were, however, not to go into effect until
Great Britain and France had agreed upon terms
of peace; and it was not until September 3, 1783,
that the definite treaty was signed. So far as
the United States was concerned Spain was left
quite properly to shift for herself.

Thus it was that the war ended. Great Britain
had urged especially the case of the Loyalists, the
return to them of their property and compensation
for their losses. She could not achieve anything.
Franklin indeed asked that Americans who had
been ruined by the destruction of their property
should be compensated by Britain, that Canada
should be added to the United States, and that
Britain should acknowledge her fault in distressing
the colonies. In the end the American Commissioners agreed to ask the individual States to meet
the desires of the British negotiators, but both
sides understood that the States would do nothing, that the confiscated property would never be

returned, that most of the exiled Loyalists would
remain exiles, and that Britain herself must com-
pensate them for their losses.   This in time she
did on a scale inadequate indeed but expressive
of a generous intention.   The United States re-
tained the great Northwest and the Mississippi
became the western frontier, with destiny already whispering that weak and grasping Spain
must soon let go of the farther West stretching
to the Pacific Ocean.   When Great Britain signed
peace with France and Spain in January, 1783,
Gibraltar was not returned; Spain had to be content with the return of Minorca and Florida which
she had been forced to yield to Britain in 1763.
Each side restored its conquests in the West Indies.
France, the chief mainstay of the war during its
later years, gained from it really nothing beyond
the weakening of her ancient enemy.   The magnanimity of France, especially towards her exacting
American ally, is one of the fine things in the great
combat.   The huge sum of nearly eight hundred
million dollars spent by France in the war was one
of the chief factors in the financial crisis which, six
years after the signing of the peace, brought on
the French Revolution and with it the overthrow
of the Bourbon monarchy.   Politics bring strange

18

bedfellows and they have rarely brought stranger ones than the democracy of young America and the political despotism, linked with idealism, of the ancient monarchy of France.

The British did not evacuate New York until Carleton had gathered there the Loyalists who claimed his protection. These unhappy people made their way to the seaports, often after long and distressing journeys overland. Charleston was the chief rallying place in the South and from there many sad-hearted people sailed away, never to see again their former homes. The British had captured New York in September, 1776, and it was more than seven years later, on November 25, 1783, that the last of the British fleet put to sea. Britain and America had broken forever their political tie and for many years to come embittered memories kept up the alienation.

It was fitting that Washington should bid farewell to his army at New York, the center of his hopes and anxieties during the greater part of the long struggle. On December 4, 1783, his officers met at a tavern to bid him farewell. The tears ran down his cheeks as he parted with these brave and tried men. He shook their hands in silence and, in a fashion still preserved in France, kissed each of them. Then they watched him as he was rowed away in his barge to the New Jersey shore. Congress was now sitting at Annapolis in Maryland and there on December 23, 1783, Washington appeared and gave up finally his command. We are told that the members sat covered to show the sovereignty of the Union, a quaint touch of the thought of the time. The little town made a brave show and "the gallery was filled with a beautiful group of elegant ladies." With solemn sincerity Washington commended the country to the protection of Almighty God and the army to the special care of Congress. Passion had already subsided for the President of Congress in his reply praised the "magnanimous king and nation" of Great Britain. By the end of the year Washington was at Mount Vernon, hoping now to be able, as he said simply, to make and sell a little flour annually and to repair houses fast going to ruin. He did not foresee the troubled years and the vexing problems which still lay before him. Nor could he, in his modest estimate of himself, know that for a distant posterity his character and his words would have compelling authority. What Washington's countryman, Motley, said of William of Orange is true of Washington himself: "As long as he lived he was the guiding star of a brave nation and when he died the little children cried in the streets." But this is not all. To this day in the domestic and foreign affairs of the United States the words of Washington, the policies which he favored, have a living and almost binding force. This attitude of mind is not without its dangers, for nations require to make new adjustments of policy, and the past is only in part the master of the present; but it is the tribute of a grateful nation to the noble character of its chief founder.

BIBLIOGRAPHICAL NOTE

In Winsor, *Narrative and Critical History of America*, vol. vi (1889), and in Larned (editor), *Literature of American History*, pp. 111–152 (1902), the authorities are critically estimated. There are excellent classified lists in Van Tyne, *The American Revolution* (1905), vol. v of Hart (editor), *The American Nation*, and in Avery, *History of the United States*, vol. v, pp. 422–432, and vol. vi, pp. 445–471 (1908–09). The notes in Channing, *A History of the United States*, vol. iii (1913), are useful. Detailed information in regard to places will be found in Lossing, *The Pictorial Field Book of the Revolution*, 2 vols. (1850).

In recent years American writers on the period have chiefly occupied themselves with special studies, and the general histories have been few. Tyler's *The Literary History of the American Revolution*, 2 vols. (1897), is a penetrating study of opinion. Fiske's *The American Revolution*, 2 vols. (1891), and Sydney George Fisher's *The Struggle for American Independence*, 2 vols. (1908), are popular works. The short volume of Van Tyne is based upon extensive research. The attention of English writers has been drawn in an increasing degree to the Revolution. Lecky, *A History of England in the Eighteenth Century*, chaps. xiii, xiv, and xv (1903), is impartial. The most elaborate and readable history is Trevelyan, *The American Revolution*, and his *George the Third* and *Charles Fox* (six volumes ir all, completed in 1914). If Trevelyan leans too much to the American side the opposite is true of Fortescue, *A History of the British Army*, vol. III (1902), a scientific account of military events with many maps and plans. Captain Mahan, U. S. N., wrote the British naval history of the period in Clowes (editor), *The Royal Navy, a History*, vol. III, pp. 353–564 (1898). Of great value also is Mahan's *Influence of Sea Power on History* (1890) and *Major Operations of the Navies in the War of Independence* (1913). He may be supplemented by C. O. Paullin's *Navy of the American Revolution* (1906) and G. W. Allen's *A Naval History of the American Revolution*, 2 vols. (1913).

CHAPTERS I AND II

Washington's own writings are necessary to an understanding of his character. Sparks, *The Life and Writings of George Washington*, 2 vols. (completed 1855), has been superseded by Ford, *The Writings of George Washington*, 14 vols. (completed 1893). The general reader will probably put aside the older biographies of Washington by Marshall, Irving, and Sparks for more recent Lives such as those by Woodrow Wilson, Henry Cabot Lodge, and Paul Leicester Ford. Haworth, *George Washington, Farmer* (1915) deals with a special side of Washington's character. The problems of the army are described in Bolton, *The Private Soldier under Washington* (1902), and in Hatch, *The Administration of the American Revolutionary Army* (1904). For military operations Frothingham, *The*

Siege of Boston; Justin H. Smith, *Our Struggle for the Fourteenth Colony*, 2 vols. (1907); Codman, *Arnold's Expedition to Quebec* (1901); and Lucas, *History of Canada, 1763–1812* (1909).

CHAPTER III

For the state of opinion in England, the contemporary *Annual Register*, and the writings and speeches of men of the time like Burke, Fox, Horace Walpole, and Dr. Samuel Johnson. The King's attitude is found in Donne, *Correspondence of George III with Lord North, 1768–83*, 2 vols. (1867). Stirling, *Coke of Norfolk and his Friends*, 2 vols. (1908), gives the outlook of a Whig magnate; Fitzmaurice, *Life of William, Earl of Shelburne*, 2 vols. (1912), the Whig policy. Curwen's *Journals and Letters, 1775–84* (1842), show us a Loyalist exile in England. Hazelton's *The Declaration of Independence, its History* (1906), is an elaborate study.

CHAPTERS IV, V, AND VI

The three campaigns — New York, Philadelphia, and the Hudson — are covered by C. F. Adams. *Studies Military and Diplomatic* (1911), which makes severe strictures on Washington's strategy; H. P. Johnston's "Campaign of 1776 around New York and Brooklyn," in the Long Island Historical Society's *Memoirs*, and *Battle of Harlem Heights* (1897); Carrington, *Battles of the American Revolution* (1904); Stryker, *The Battles of Trenton and Princeton* (1898); Lucas, *History of Canada* (1909). Fonblanque's *John Burgoyne* (1876) is a defense of that leader; while Riedesel's

Letters and Journals Relating to the War of the American Revolution (trans. W. L. Stone, 1867) and Anburey's *Travels through the Interior Parts of America* (1789) are accounts by eye-witnesses. Mereness' (editor) *Travels in the American Colonies, 1690–1783* (1916) gives the impressions of Lord Adam Gordon and others.

CHAPTERS VII AND VIII

On Washington at Valley Forge, Oliver, *Life of Alexander Hamilton* (1906); Charlemagne Tower, *The Marquis de La Fayette in the American Revolution*, 2 vols. (1895); Greene, *Life of Nathanael Greene* (1893); Brooks, *Henry Knox* (1900); Graham, *Life of General Daniel Morgan* (1856); Kapp, *Life of Steuben* (1859); Arnold, *Life of Benedict Arnold* (1880). On the army Bolton and Hatch as cited; Mahan gives a lucid account of naval effort. Barrow, *Richard, Earl Howe* (1838) is a dull account of a remarkable man. On the French alliance, Perkins, *France in the American Revolution* (1911), Corwin, *French Policy and the American Alliance of 1778* (1916), and Van Tyne on "Influences which Determined the French Government to Make the Treaty with America, 1778," in *The American Historical Review*, April, 1916.

CHAPTER IX

Fortescue, as cited, gives excellent plans. Other useful books are McCrady, *History of South Carolina in the Revolution* (1901); Draper, *King's Mountain and its Heroes* (1881); Simms, *Life of Marion* (1844). Ross (editor), *The Cornwallis Correspondence*, 3 vols. (1859), and Tarleton, *History of the Campaigns of 1780 and 1781 in the Southern Provinces of North America* (1787), give the point of view of British leaders. On the West, Thwaites, *How George Rogers Clark won the Northwest* (1903); and on the Loyalists Van Tyne, *The Loyalists in the American Revolution* (1902), Flick, *Loyalism in New York* (1901), and Stark, *The Loyalists of Massachusetts* (1910).

CHAPTERS X AND XI

For the exploits of John Paul Jones and of the American navy, Mrs. De Koven's *The Life and Letters of John Paul Jones*, 2 vols. (1913), Don C. Seitz's *Paul Jones*, and G. W. Allen's *A Naval History of the American Revolution*, 2 vols. (1913), should be consulted. Jusserand's *With Americans of Past and Present Days* (1917) contains a chapter on "Rochambeau and the French in America"; Johnston's *The Yorktown Campaign* (1881) is a full account; Wraxall, *Historical Memoirs of my own Time* (1815, reprinted 1904), tells of the reception of the news of Yorktown in England.

The Encyclopædia Britannica has useful references to authorities for persons prominent in the Revolution and *The Dictionary of National Biography* for leaders on the British side.

INDEX

A

Abraham, Plains of, American army on, 50

Adams, Abigail, 49

Adams, John, in Continental Congress, 8; journey from Boston to Philadelphia, 9–10; on committee to draft Declaration of Independence, 75–76; excepted from British offer of pardon, 86, 92; opinion of Philadelphia, 120, 165; criticism of Washington, 149; sent to Paris on American Commission, 270–271

Albany (N. Y.), plan to concentrate British forces at, 133

Allen, Colonel Ethan, 40

André, Major John, at Philadelphia, 195; treats with Arnold, 241–42; capture, 242–43; hanged as spy, 243

Annapolis (Md.), Congress at, 275

Anne, Fort, 129

Armed neutrality, 206

Army, American, camp at Cambridge, 27–28; Washington reorganizes, 30–35; food and clothing, 30–31, 32, 153–56, 166; composition, 31–32, 43; officers, 32–35, 43–44; after Canadian campaign, 51; desertions, 100, 159–60; plundering by, 111; pay, 111, 158–59, 209; in 1777, 112; condition under Gates, 145; Washington wishes national, 151; need of engineers, 152; hospital service, 152–53, 166–67; weapons and artillery, 156–158; religion in, 160–61; supplies from France, 184; after Valley Forge, 197; mutinous, 209, 246

Army, British, food for, 36; press-gangs, 176; flogging, 176; relations between officers and men, 176–77; difficulties of raising, 178; *see also* Germans

Army, French, in America, 235–36

Arnold, Benedict, at Ticonderoga, 40; through Maine to Canada, 43, 44–45; at Quebec, 45–46; at Crown Point, 52–53; Coke denounces King's reception of, 71; Washington's trust in, 110, 172–73; at Stillwater, 143; describes American army, 155; treason, 173, 195, 240–43; at West Point, 238; life at Philadelphia, 239; tried by court-martial, 239; reprimanded by Washington, 239–40; in Virginia, 251

Articles of Confederation, 163

Assanpink River, Washington on, 105

Atrocities, 180, 212; *see also* Indians, Prisons

Augusta (Ga.), British take, 211–12; falls to Americans, 250

B

Baltimore, Congress flees to, 100
Barbados, Washington visits, 22
Barras, French naval commander, 261
Baum, Colonel, at Bennington, 131, 132
Beaumarchais sends munitions to America, 183–84
Bemis Heights, battle, 143
Bennington, battle of, 131–32
Berthier, French officer, 231
Biggin's Bridge, Tarleton's victory at, 216
Bordentown, Germans at, 102
Boston, defiance of British in, 2; siege, 3, 4, 35–36; Washington's journey to, 9–10; American camp, 27–28; evacuated by British, 48–49; effect of Washington's success at, 81; Howe feigns setting out for, 114; safe, 116; Burgoyne's force at, 146; Loyalists in, 212
Braddock, General Edward, Washington with, 22–23
Brandywine, battle of, 119–20, 133, 148; La Fayette at, 169; Greene at, 171
Brant, Joseph (Thayendanegea), 134
Breed's Hill, 4–5; see also Bunker Hill
Broglie, Comte de, suggested as commander of American army, 185
Broglie, Prince de, with French army in America, 232
Brooklyn Heights, Washington on, 88–91
Buford, Colonel, Tarleton attacks, 217

Bunker Hill, battle of, 4–7, 33; Washington learns of, 10; significance, 21; officers at, 33, 35
Burgoyne, General John, on British behavior at Bunker Hill, 7; ordered to meet Howe, 68, 112, 113, 124–25; Howe deserts, 116, 130; life and character, 123–24; at Lake Champlain, 125 et seq.; Indian Allies, 125–26, 138–140, 144; takes Fort Ticonderoga, 127; lack of supplies, 129–30; at Fort Edward, 129, 130, 141; and Bennington, 131–32; at Saratoga, 132, 141, 143; learns of failure of St. Leger, 136; crosses Hudson, 141; at Stillwater (Freeman's Farm), 142–43; surrender at Saratoga, 68, 122, 143–47, 149; condition of army, 144; effect on France of surrender of, 186; effect of surrender in England, 190, 192
Burke, Edmund, and conciliation, 69; and Independence, 190
Byron, Admiral, sent to aid Howe, 200

C

Cahokia, Clark at, 223
Cambridge, American camp, 3, 27–28; Washington at, 10, 30–31, 34, 35, 146
Camden, battle of, 219–20, 236
Canada, campaign against, 37, 38–47; Washington's idea of, 40; France and, 188; Loyalists take refuge in, 227–28
Carleton, Sir Guy, Governor of Canada, 42; commands at Quebec, 45–46; operations on Lake Champlain, 52–53; Howe and, 95; superseded

Carleton, Sir Guy—*Continued*
by Burgoyne, 124; commands at New York, 269; and Loyalists, 274

Carroll, Charles, of Carrollton, on commission to Montreal, 50

Carroll, John, on commission to Montreal, 50

Catherine II advises England against war, 179

Catholics, Quebec Act, 38–39, 41; disabilities in England, 208

Chadd's Ford, Washington at, 118, 119

Champlain, Lake, plan for conquest of Canada by way of, 43; operations on, 52–53, 95; Burgoyne at, 125 *et seq.*; Arnold at, 238

Charleston (S. C.), on side of Revolution, 37; British expedition to, 82–83; Prevost demands surrender, 213–14; Lincoln at, 215–17, surrenders, 217

Charlestown (Mass.), location, 3; burned, 5, 7

Charlotte (N. C.), Greene at, 247

Charlottesville (Va.), Cornwallis plans raid of, 252

Chatham, William Pitt, Earl of, and conciliation with America, 69, 190; political status, 192, 193

Cherry Valley, massacre, 229

Chesapeake Bay, Howe on, 116, 117; *see also* Yorktown

Chew, Benjamin, house as central point in battle at Germantown, 122

Clark, G. R., expedition, 223

Clinton, General Sir Henry, 230; at Charleston, 82, 215; at New York, 116, 130, 133; up the Hudson, 143, 145; succeeds Howe in command,

195; march from Philadelphia, 196, 197, 198; retreats at Monmouth Court House, 199; reaches Newport, 202; sails for Charleston, 217–18; proclamation, 218; Rodney relieves, 237; and Cornwallis, 253; delay in reinforcing Cornwallis, 262–63, 265

Coke of Norfolk, wealth, 20, 69–70; and Toryism, 70–71; on American question, 71–72; and Washington, 71, 72, 189

Colonies, attitude toward England, 55 *et seq.*; state of society in, 60; population, 177–78; *see also* names of colonies

Continental Congress, Washington at, 1, 259; selects leader for army, 7–9; Howe's conciliation, 92–93; flees to Baltimore, 100; loses able men, 110; hampers Washington, 110; Gates and, 142; repudiates Gates's terms to Burgoyne, 146; Gates lays quarrel with Washington before, 150; and enlistment, 151; at York, 162, 163; ineptitude, 163–64, 236, 269–270; gives Southern command to Gates, 219; Test Acts, 226; and French alliance, 244; borrows money from France, 271; at Annapolis, 275

Conway, General, and Stamp Act, 69

Conway, General Thomas, 110; "Conway Cabal" against Washington, 149, 150; leaves America, 151

Cornwallis, Lord, 230; at Charleston, 82; crosses Hudson, 97; goes to Trenton, 104–105; at Princeton, 106; and

Cornwallis, Lord—*Continued*
Howe, 115; at the Brandy-
wine, 119; goes to Charleston,
216; at Camden, 219; in
North Carolina, 221, 247–
248; proclamation, 249;
Guilford Court House, 249;
advance down Cape Fear
River, 250; in Virginia, 251–
252; and Clinton, 253; Yorktown, 254 *et seq.*; surrender,
264–66
Countess of Scarborough (ship),
Jones captures, 205
Cowpens, battle of, 172, 248
Cromwell, Oliver, as military
leader, 170
Crown Point, capture of, 52–
53; Burgoyne at, 126

D

Dartmouth, Earl of, Minister
of England, 63
Deane, Silas, envoy to France,
184–85
Declaration of Independence,
75–80
Delaware Bay, British fleet in,
116
Delaware River, Washington
crosses, 102
Denmark and armed neutrality, 206–07
Detroit, force to check Clark
from, 223
Devonshire, Duke of, costly
residence, 18
Dickinson, John, of Pennsylvania, on Declaration of
Independence, 78
Dilworth, Cornwallis marches
on, 119
Dinwiddie, Governor, Washington and, 16
Donop, Count von, at Trenton,
102, 104
Dorchester Heights, American
troops on, 47–48

Dumas, French officer with
Rochambeau, 231
Dunmɔre, Lord, Governor of
Virginia, 224

E

East River, location, 87; British on, 93
Edward, Fort, St. Clair retires
to, 127; Burgoyne at, 129,
130–141; Indian raids at,
140; Burgoyne seeks to return to, 143
Elkton, Howe at, 116, 118;
American army at, 258
Emerson, chaplain, diary
quoted, 35
England, in eighteenth century, 16–19; state of society,
19, 59; Parliament votes tax
on colonies, 23; politics, 24–
25, 64 *et seq.*, 268; attitude
toward colonies, 54–55, 58;
prosperity, 59; difficulties in
raising army, 178; France
and, 182–83, 187–88, 191–
192, 195–96, 206, 270; Whig
attitude after French intervention, 189–90; and Spain,
187, 203–204, 206; navy in
1779, 204; domestic affairs,
207; treaty of peace, 272;
see also Army, British
Estaing, Count d', French
admiral, 195; at the Delaware, 196–97; at Sandy
Hook, 200–01; at Newport,
201–02; at Savannah, 214–
215
Eutaw Springs, battle of, 250

F

Falmouth (Portland) (Me.),
destroyed, 81
Ferguson, Major Patrick, 216;
King's Mountain, 221–22;
killed, 222

Fersen, Count, with French army, 232
Finance, value of continental money, 209; Franklin procures money in France, 271
Florida returned to Spain, 273
Foch, General, quoted, 101
Fox, C. J., and carelessness of ministers, 68; urges conciliation, 69
France, French in Canada, 38; alliance with, 182 et seq.; and England, 182-83, 187-188, 191-92, 195-96, 206, 270; treaty of friendship with America (1778), 187; and Canada, 188; and Spain, 203; promises soldiers to Washington, 210; help in 1780, 230 et seq.; bibliography of alliance, 280
Franklin, Benjamin, on Lexington, 2; on George III, 25; member of commission to Montreal, 50; on committee to meet Howe, 93; satirizes British ignorance, 138; in Congress, 164; induces Hessians to desert, 180; sent to Paris, 185; and Loyalists, 225, 270, 271
Fraser, General, killed, 143
Frederick the Great, of Prussia, estimate of Washington, 105; urges France against England, 187

G

Gage, General Thomas, 72; at Boston, 3, 4-5
Gates, General Horatio, 98, 110, 172, 173; in command of Lee's army, 99-100; joins Washington, 100; discourages Washington, 103; against Burgoyne, 142-45; intrigue, 149-51; menaces

Clinton in New Jersey, 198; command in the South, 219; Camden, 219; Greene supersedes, 247
George III, American opinions of, 25; Hamilton on, 39; character, 60-62; speech in Parliament, 62-63; Washington and, 63, 86; statue destroyed in New York, 80; ready to give guarantees of liberty, 115; effect of news of Ticonderoga on, 127-28; on taxing of America, 190; and Chatham, 193; news of Yorktown, 267-68
George, Fort, Burgoyne's supplies from, 129
Georgia, British in, 211-12, 217
Germain, Lord George, failure to send orders to Howe, 68, 125; instructions to Burgoyne, 112; plans campaign from England, 130-31; censures Howe, 194; in Seven Years' War, 230; news of Yorktown, 267
Germans, hold line of the Delaware, 102; plundering, 111; at Bennington, 131-32; with Burgoyne, 144, 145; Steuben's part in Revolutionary War, 174-76; benefit to British, 179-80; desertions, 180-81, 199
Germantown, Howe's camp at, 121; battle of, 122, 148; Greene at, 171
Gibraltar, Spain besieges, 270; not returned to Spain, 273
Gloucester, Cornwallis holds, 263
Gordon, Lord Adam, on Philadelphia, 120; opinion of Charleston, 215
Gordon, Lord George, leads London riot, 208
Grasse, Comte de, commands French fleet, 256; at Chesa-

Grasse, Comte de—*Continued*
peake Bay, 260, 261–62;
sails south, 265; Rodney
captures, 266, 270
Great Britain, *see* England
Greene, General Nathanael,
110; at Bunker Hill, 4; ad-
vocates independence, 75;
commands Fort Washing-
ton, 96–97; harasses Cornwallis, 105; at Germantown,
122; at Valley Forge, 170–
171; in Rhode Island, 201; on
Congress, 236; supersedes
Gates in South, 247; Guilford Court House, 249; at
Hobkirk's Hill, 250
Grey, Sir Charles, Howe and,
115
Guilford Court House, 249

H

Hamilton, Alexander, 238; and
Washington, 16, 168; on
Quebec Act, 39
Hancock, John, desires post as
Commander-in-Chief, 8
Harlem River, location, 87
Hastings, Marquis of, 6; *see
also* Rawdon, Lord
Henry, Patrick, speech, 57
Henry, Cape, naval battle off,
261
Herkimer, General Nicholas,
battle of Oriskany, 135
Hessians, *see* Germans
Hillsborough (N. C.), Corn-
wallis issues proclamation
at, 249
Hobkirk's Hill, Rawdon de-
feats Greene at, 250
Holkham, Lord Leicester's
residence at, 18; Coke's res-
idence at, 69–70, 71
Holland joins England's ene-
mies, 206, 246
Hood, Sir Samuel, British ad-
miral, 261

Howe, Richard, Lord, com-
mands fleet reaching New
York, 84, 86; Whig sym-
pathy, 85; personal characteristics, 85; letter to Washington, 86–87; seeks' peace,
92–93; takes fleet to Newport, 100; proclamation, 101;
and evacuation of Philadelphia, 196–97; expects naval
fight off Sandy Hook, 200–
201; at Newport, 202; re-
fuses to serve Tory Ad-
miralty, 207
Howe, General Sir William, at
Bunker Hill, 5; succeeds
Gage in command, 5, 36;
evacuates Boston, 47–48;
and Burgoyne, 68, 112, 116–
117, 130, 142; personal characteristics, 84; attitude toward Revolution, 84; lands
army on Staten Island, 86;
battle of Long Island, 87–
90; in New York, 93–95;
plans to meet Carleton, 95;
battle of White Plains, 96;
Fort Washington, 96–97;
takes Fort Lee, 98; and Lee,
99, 112–13; at Trenton, 100;
proclamation, 101, 111; goes
to New York for Christmas,
102; dilatoriness, 109, 110;
takes Philadelphia, 109, 112,
120, 149; plan of 1777, 112–
113; sails for Chesapeake
Bay, 115–16; at the Brandywine, 118–19, 133; and
Pennsylvanians, 120–21; at
Germantown, 121–22; leaves
Philadelphia, 194; Clinton
succeeds, 195
Hudson River, advantages of
plan to sail up, 82; location of mouth, 87; British
on, 93, 96–98; Washing-
ton guards, 209–10, 211,
236, 237–38; *see also* West
Point

I

Independence, 54 *et seq.*; *see also* Declaration of Independence
Independence, Fort, 127
India, France against British in, 206
Indians, allies of Burgoyne, 125, 133, 138, 139-40, 144; with St. Leger, 134-36; aid Loyalists in Wyoming massacre, 229
Ireland, Declaration of Independence, 208

J

Jay, John, on Declaration of Independence, 78; opinion of Congress, 162; on American Commission, 270
Jefferson, Thomas, and Declaration of Independence, 75-77; on La Fayette, 170; British plan to capture, 252
Johnson, Sir John, with St. Leger, 133-34, 135
Johnson, Samuel, quoted, 58
Johnson, Sir William, 134
Jones, John Paul, 204-06; bibliography, 281

K

Kalb, Baron de, part in Revolutionary War, 173-74; killed, 220
Kaskaskia, Clark at, 223
Kenneth Square, British camp at, 118
Keppel, Admiral, and London riots, 207
King's Mountain, battle of, 221-22
Knox, Henry, Washington values service of, 110, 171-172

Knyphausen, General, and Howe, 115; at the Brandywine, 118; effective service, 179-80
Kosciuszko, in American army, 173

L

La Fayette, Marquis de, 182, 230, 238; and Washington, 13, 168, 169; and independence of America, 30; personal characteristics, 169-170; volunteers through Deane's influence, 185; with Lee at Monmouth Court House, 198-99; sent to France (1779), 210; as interpreter for Washington and Rochambeau, 234; in Virginia, 251-52
Lansdowne, Marquis of, *see* Shelburne, Lord
Laurens, Henry, on American Commission, 270
Lauzun, Duc de, with French army in America, 231-32, 233
Laval-Montmorency, French officer in America, 232
Lee, Arthur, on commission to Paris, 185
Lee, General Charles, 150, 172; Washington writes to, 30; at Fort Washington, 98; disobeys Washington, 98-99; letter to Gates, 99; captured, 99; and Howe, 99, 112-13; freed by exchange of prisoners, 173; personal characteristics, 173; and training of recruits, 176; at Monmouth Court House, 198-199; court-martialed, 199; suspended, 199; dismissed from army, 199
Lee, R. H., and Declaration of Independence, 75

10

Lee, Fort, 96; Washington at, 97; falls to British, 97, 98

Leicester, Lord, costly residence at Holkham, 18

Lexington, battle of, 2, 21

Lincoln, Abraham, quoted, 29; and Declaration of Independence, 76, 77–78

Lincoln, General Benjamin, at Ticonderoga, 142; southern campaign, 214, 215, 217, 264

Long Island, battle of, 87–90, 91

Loyalists, Howe and Pennsylvania, 162; plundering, 203, 228; in South, 212–13; Clinton's proclamation to, 218; decline in strength, 224; punishments, 225–26; Test Acts, 226; question of compensation of, 272; gather in New York to claim British protection, 274; bibliography, 281

Luzerne, French Minister, 258

M

McCrae, Jeannie, carried off by Indians, 140

McNeil, Mrs., carried off by Indians, 140

Maine, Arnold's expedition, 43, 44

Marie Antoinette, Queen, zeal for liberal ideas, 183; Fersen friend of, 232

Marion, Francis, guerrilla leader, 220, 247

Marlborough, Duke of, costly residence, 18

Martha's Vineyard, Loyalist refugees plunder, 228

Maryland, and independence, 75; Howe plans to secure control of, 113

Massachusetts, Suffolk County defies England, 28–29; North and constitution of, 191; list of Loyalists, 226

Minorca returned to Spain, 273

Mirabeau, French officer in America, 232

Mississippi River becomes western frontier of United States, 273

Monmouth Court House, battle of, 198–99; Lee at, 176

Montgomery, General Richard, expedition to Canada, 43; at Quebec, 45–46; death, 46–47, 98

Montreal, Montgomery enters, 44; Commission sent to, 50; evacuated, 51; St. Leger reaches, 136

Morgan, Captain Daniel, at Quebec, 46; with Greene, 247; at Cowpens, 248

Morris, Gouverneur, opinion of Congress, 162

Morristown (N. J.), American headquarters at, 99, 106, 110

Moultrie, Fort, battle at, 83

Mount Vernon, Washington's estate, 20, 259, 275

Murray, Mrs., saves Putnam's army, 94

N

Narragansett Bay, British blockade French fleet in, 234

Navy, American, Jones and, 204–06; need for supremacy, 231

Navy, British, condition in 1779, 204; factions, 207

Necessity, Fort, surrender of, 148

New Bedford, Loyalists burn, 228

New England, question of leader from, 8; and Washington, 11; character of

New England—*Continued*
people, 29; equality in, 33;
on independence, 75; revolutionary, 81; and Indians,
137; and Burgoyne, 145;
States jealous of, 164–65

New Hampshire offers bounty
for Indian scalps, 137–38

New Jersey, Washington's
flight across, 97, 100; Lee
retreats to, 99; loyalty,
110; Howe's proclamation,
110; Washington recovers,
106; Howe moves across, 110,
114; Clinton crosses, 196,
197

New York, on independence,
75; Howe's proclamation,
101; Howe's plan to hold,
113; acquires Loyalist lands,
228

New York City, on side of
Revolution, 37; Washington
plans to hold, 37–38; loss of,
52, 81 *et seq.*, 108, 148;
statue of King destroyed,
80; burned, 94–95; Wash-
ington plans march to, 116;
for naval defence, 195;
Loyalists take refuge in,
227; French army moves
toward, 253; Washington
returns to, 269; Washington
bids farewell to army at, 274

Newgate jail burned, 208

Newport, Lord Howe's fleet
at, 100; British hold, 201;
French fleet sails into, 233;
French army leaves, 253

Noailles, Vicomte de, on foot
from Newport to Yorktown,
259

Norfolk (Va.), destroyed, 81

North, Lord, Prime Minister,
63–64, 190–91; George III
writes to, 61; seeks to retire,
192, 193; and news of Yorktown, 267; resigns, 268

North Carolina, and independence, 75; campaign in, 247–
251

Northwest, United States re-
tains, 273

Nova Scotia, Washington's
belief of sympathy in, 42;
Loyalists go to, 227

O

Ogg, F. A., *The Old Northwest*,
cited, 224 (note)

Oriskany, battle of, 135

P

Paine, Thomas, 74; *Common
Sense*, 75

Palliser, Sir Hugh, and British
naval quarrel, 207

Panther, Wyandot chief, shows
scalp of Miss McCrae, 140

Parker, Admiral Sir Peter,
before Fort Moultrie, 82–83

Pennsylvania, and independence, 75; loyalty, 101;
Howe plans to secure con-
trol of, 113; "Black List" of
Loyalists, 226

Percy, Earl, opinion of rebels
in America, 32

Petersburg (Va.), Arnold at,
251

Philadelphia, second Con-
tinental Congress at, 1, 7–9;
Washington sets out from,
9; on side of Revolution, 37;
Paine in, 74; Howe plans to
secure, 100, 101; loss of, 108
et seq., 148; Howe leaves,
194; Mischianza in, 194–95;
British abandon, 196; Loyalists hanged in, 226; Arnold
in command at, 238; French
army reviewed in, 257–58

Pigot, General, at Newport,
201

Pitt, William, *see* Chatham.
Earl of

Politics, *see* England

Prescott, Colonel, at Bunker Hill, 4

Preston, Major, British officer at St. Johns, 44

Prevost, General Augustine, at Charleston, 213–14

Prices, 167

Princeton, Cornwallis at, 106

Prisons, British prison-ships, 153; London riots, 208

Privateers, checked at Newport, 100; France and, 186

Providence (R. I.), Greene and Sullivan at, 201

Putnam, Israel, at Bunker Hill, 4, 6; leaves New York, 94

Q

Quebec, Arnold and Montgomery before, 45–46, 49–50, 82, 98, 238; Morgan at, 172, 247

Quebec Act, 38–39, 41

R

Rahl, Colonel, at Trenton, 102; killed, 104

Rawdon, Lord Francis, at Bunker Hill, 6; at Camden, 219, 250

Reed, Joseph, charge against Arnold, 239

Revolutionary War, bibliography, 277–78

Rhode Island, British control, 100; Washington's campaign against, 201–02; British evacuate, 211

Richmond, Duke of, opinion of Revolution, 69

Richmond (Va.), Arnold burns, 251

Riedesel, General, at Lake Champlain, 125; effective service to British, 179–80

Riedesel, Baroness, reports conditions in New England, 137

Rochambeau, Comte de, leader of French army in America, 230–31; idea of naval supremacy, 231, 255; and Washington, 234, 236, 237; on American situation (1781), 246; goes to Yorktown, 258; in Virginia, 269

Rockingham, Marquis of, Prime Minister, 268

Rodney, Admiral, arrives in America, 236; captures St. Eustatius, 246; captures Grasse, 266, 270

Russia, British endeavor to get troops in, 179; Armed Neutrality, 206

S

St. Clair, General Arthur, a' Fort Ticonderoga, 127

St. Eustatius captured by Rodney, 246

St. Johns, Montgomery captures, 44

St. Leger, General Barry, at Fort Stanwix, 133–34; at Oriskany, 135–36

Saint-Simon, French officer in America, 232

Sandy Hook, French fleet at, 200, 201

Saratoga, Burgoyne at, 132, 141, 143; Burgoyne's surrender, 68, 122, 143–47, 149, 186; Arnold at, 238; Morgan at, 247

Savannah (Ga.), British land at, 211

Savile, Sir George, opinion of Revolution, 69

Schuyler, General Philip, goes to Canada by way of Lake Champlain, 43; Gates supersedes, 142

Serapis (ship), Jones captures, 205

Shelburne, Lord, Prime Minister, 268

Shippen, Margaret, 195; marries Arnold, 239

Simcoe, General J. G., with Clinton at Charleston, 216; Governor of Upper Canada, 228

Skinner, C. L., *Pioneers of the Old Southwest*, cited, 222 (note)

Slavery, Washington as a slave-owner, 21

Slave-trade, Declaration of Independence makes King responsible for, 77

South, war in the, 211 *et seq.*

South Carolina, neutrality proposed, 213; British control, 217

Spain, against England, 187, 203-04, 206; navy, 187; and Gibralter, 270; and peace treaty, 272

Stamp Act, 69, 183, 192

Stanwix, Fort, St. Leger before, 133-34

Staten Island, Howe on, 86, 87, 115

States, Congress and, 163

Steuben, Baron von, service in Revolution, 174-75; in Virginia, 247

Stillwater, American camp at, 141; Burgoyne attacks Gates at, 142-43; Burgoyne's defeat, 143

Stirling, Lord, prisoner, 89

Stony Point, 99

Stuart, Gilbert, and Washington, 16

Sullivan, General John, taken prisoner at battle of Long Island, 89; sent by Howe to interview Congress, 92; exchanged, 99: at Morristown, 99; and Washington, 110-11;

at Germantown, 122; at Providence, 201

Sumter, Thomas, guerrilla leader, 220, 247

Sweden, Armed Neutrality, 206

T

Talleyrand, French officer in America, 232

Tarleton, Colonel Banastre, raids, 216, 217; at Camden, 219-20; and Marion, 221; King's Mountain, 248; takes Charlottesville (Va.), 252-253; in Yorktown, 263; and Cornwallis, 264

Terrible (ship), 261

Test Acts, 226

Thayendanegea (Joseph Brant), 134

Thomas, General, on Plains of Abraham, 50

Thompson, General, attacks Three Rivers, 51

Three Rivers, attack on, 51

Throg's Neck, Howe at, 95

Ticonderoga, Fort, captured by Allen, 39-40, 42; Arnold retreats to, 53; Burgoyne lays siege to, 126-27; Lincoln besieges, 142

Tories, plundering of, 111; *see also* Loyalists

Toronto, Loyalists in, 228

Transportation, need of military engineers for, 152

Trenton, Howe at, 100; attack on, 101-07, 109; Greene at, 171

Tryon, Governor of New York, 225

V

Valley Forge, Washington at, 148 *et seq.*; Washington leaves, 196